successful

CHANGE MANAGEMENT

E.J. Lister PMC

learn to manage change
to achieve performance excellence

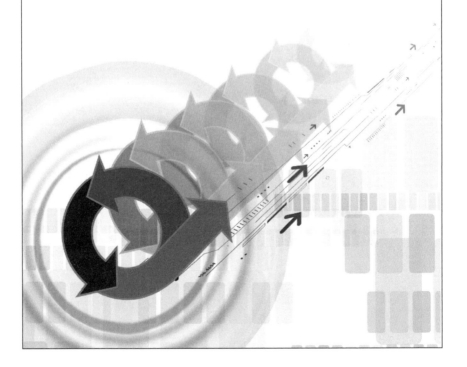

Successful Change Management

Trademarks

Change Management Process Model™
Recognition and Acceptance of Change—RAC™

National Library of Canadian Cataloguing in Publication Data

Lister, E.J. (Edmund J.), 1957-
Successful Change Management, 2nd edition
1. Organizational change. I. Title.
HD58.8I57 2001   658.4'06 C2001-910109-0
ISBN 0-9688417- 1-6

Distributed by:

Lister Management Inc.

3115 River Road
Chemainus, BC Canada V0R 1K3
Ph: 250-246-3470 Fax: 250-246-3475
tlister@listermanagement.com
order@listermanagement.com

Cover artwork by C. Greig-Manning, ConnemaraStudio
Edited by Gail Taylor, Yvonne Schmidhauser and Julie Stauffer
Production by E.J. Lister
First Printing 2003
Printed and bound in Canada by Friesens Corporation

Preface

In today's fast-paced world of competition, opportunity and uncertainty, you can't avoid change. Sometimes it's driven by need; sometimes it's driven by want. Yet many individuals and businesses find the process uncomfortable, and few achieve the results they're looking for.

Dealing with change successfully depends on understanding why it's necessary and how to manage it. That's what this book is about. It gives you a tested change process and change management tools that will support you in whatever kind of change you undertake: in your work, business or personal life. You'll learn how to eliminate the discomfort of transition and create an environment of pleasure and success, so that you can become a top achiever.

Purpose

I am passionate about change and the opportunities it provides—opportunities that have proven my change process and theories can successfully identify, manage and control change.

My purpose in writing this book is to share my acquired knowledge and experience to help you to achieve performance excellence within your personal, work or business environment.

It was difficult to cover these very different environments in one publication. At times I considered focusing solely on business change, as most of my professional colleagues have done. However, I could not ignore my belief that business change is dramatically dependent on personal recognition and acceptance of change. I believe that individuals who learn to recognize and accept change will not only enhance their personal environment, they will be better equipped to deal with change in their workplace as well. So although the primary focus of this book is on managing business change, I've included plenty of examples of personal change as well.

Whether you're looking for self-improvement, you want to lead change within your business, or you want to help employees at every level of your organization deal with change, I am confident that following the process outlined in this book will give you the results you're looking for.

This book is not based on academic reference, research or knowledge alone, but rather years of field experience, common sense, passion and desire—in my belief, the true ingredients of success.

E.J. (Ted) Lister
Lister Management Inc.

Dedication

For Toonie, the love of my life. To my wonderful family, and most affectionately to my father, who passed away suddenly before this work was finished.

Acknowledgements

I am indebted to so many people who have contributed to my personal and business successes over the years. Many of them provided me with the opportunities that created positive change in my life. It is because of their willingness to support my ambitions and share their knowledge and experiences that I am able to communicate my knowledge with others through the efforts of this book. Many thanks to my good friend Richard Mundy for the wonderful opportunity many years ago that initiated my most significant change; to Connie Manning of Connemara Studio for her enthusiasm and support in managing this project, and for her artistic contribution to its design. To Julie Stauffer, for her excellent editing, without which I would not have had the courage to distribute this work. To Dale LeTourneau, of the Chameleon Group, for her expert design and content formatting. Special thanks to Grant, creator of Grantland comics, for his permission and ability to add humor to an otherwise humorless topic.

Facilitating projects and sharing knowledge through training and coaching are a wonderful way to meet people and make new friends. Unfortunately, my contribution to each project must eventually end, but this does not mean the friendships end too. My thoughts often go back to the many people around the world I have had the pleasure to befriend and work with as a management consultant. To them I sincerely acknowledge their friendship and interest in my work. Each in their own way contributed to the contents of this book. I only hope my writing efforts reflect their wisdom well.

About the Cover

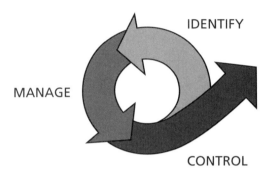

IDENTIFY

MANAGE

CONTROL

Recognition and Acceptance of Change—RAC™

The symbol on the front cover represents a change in direction away from the status quo. Although change is constant, it's difficult to break away from the circle of comfort without recognizing and accepting change.

I encourage you to think about this symbol and remember what it represents as you go about your daily routine. Choose to break away from the status quo and look for opportunities to redirect and improve. Choose the direction you travel by embracing change. Life will not permit you to circle in comfort forever. Better you choose than let life's events make the choice for you.

How to Use This Book

Perhaps you need help pinpointing opportunities for improvement at work, or you have identified a poor business practice but you're not sure how to manage the transition to best practices. Maybe you have volunteered or been chosen to take part in a change improvement project, or you're dealing with an unexpected change event and you're looking for help to manage and adapt. Perhaps you've identified a need to change a personal situation to improve your quality of life.

Whatever your reason, this book will help you manage change successfully. Think of this as a workbook and reference book combined—a hands-on guide to learning a new Change Management Process, and a reference guide you can turn to throughout your change improvement project.

Part One discusses the concept of change and introduces you to the Change Management Process Model. Part Two walks you through the model step by step, with lots of helpful examples. Part Three is for businesses, looking at how change can affect the structure of an organization, while Part Four consists of three real-life case studies involving personal and business change. I encourage you to take the time to read each chapter and become familiar with all the material before you begin managing your change, regardless of your current situation.

Once you've read the book and launched your change improvement project, you can use the checklists at the end of each chapter to ensure that you've understood and executed each step in the pursuit of successful change.

Contents

Part I INTRODUCTION
Chapter 1: Understanding Change

Chapter 2: Model Overview

Part II CHANGE MANAGEMENT PROCESS
(A) PLANNING PHASE
Chapter 3: Identification

Chapter 4: Establishment

(B) DEVELOPMENT PHASE

Chapter 5: Methodology

Chapter 6: Design

(C) IMPLEMENTATION PHASE

Chapter 7: Orientation and Training

Chapter 7 Checklist: Orientation and Training

Chapter 8: Roll-Out

Chapter 8 Checklist: Roll-out

(D) MANAGEMENT PHASE

Chapter 9: Control and Coaching

Part IV CASE STUDIES

Chapter 12: Manufacturing—A Case Study

Chapter 13: Service—A Case Study

Chapter 14: Personal Change—A Case Study

Part V APPENDIX

Part I INTRODUCTION

Chapter 1
Understanding Change

"There is nothing more difficult to carry out, nor more doubtful of success, nor more dangerous to handle, than to initiate a new order of things. For the former has enemies in all who profit by the old order, and lukewarm defenders in all those who would profit by the new order."

Niccolo Machiavelli

The dictionary describes change as the act, process, or result of changing. However, most people describe it as the act of creating discomfort, mainly because without a defined process, the result of changing is often uncertain. So naturally they resist it. Do any of the following comments sound familiar?

"I don't see anything wrong with the way we are currently doing things around here. Why do we have to change?"

"We have tried to change the way our people perform their routine daily activities with the goal of becoming more efficient, but it was like asking them to walk on hot coals."

"I've tried to change personal habits, but it doesn't work—I never achieve my desired results."

"Our managers implement changes without really understanding what it is we do."

"Our company doesn't seem to have a clear vision of the future. We just react to change, and the results often aren't successful."

Sometimes it's hard to imagine how humans have come as far as we have with such a lack of enthusiasm for change. However, with our tested Change Management Process, you *can* accept it and adapt it—and then reap the benefits.

This book explores the concepts of change from a perspective of improvement and opportunity. You'll learn how to see problems and opportunities, how to create change to improve current practices, and how to adapt to change in your personal life, your workplace or your business. The secret to successful change is *management* of change.

Why Change is Necessary

All around us, things are constantly changing. Some of these changes occur naturally, while others are initiated by something that we do or other people do.

Natural change is simply the result of living: the seasons change, we grow older and things around us evolve. Sometimes we create positive changes through our own actions, such as improving our health by exercising more often, acquiring wealth by investing more wisely, or working our way to a better job. Sometimes we make poor choices that lead in quite the opposite direction, to problems such as poor health, loss of income, or loss of a job. Other people can affect our personal, work or business life in much the same way.

In my life I have experienced all of the problems and opportunities I've just described, and learned a lot in the process.

> *When I was 19, I purchased a piece of rural property with the dream of building a log home and settling down to a peaceful life with an adorable wife and children. I married a beautiful woman who shared my dream, and together we began making plans. We moved to a small town near to our property and I began to look for work. After months of struggling to find a job, it became obvious that my wife would have to be the one to support us through the first winter. She took a job as a front desk manager for a large hotel*

chain. We lived in a small apartment in a less than desirable part of town. The winter was long and hard, my old truck was losing its will to live, and I was beginning to lose mine.

I kept myself busy, however, by drafting the plans for our house. I realized that my dream of a log home wasn't very realistic, so I took my father's advice and began to draw plans for a three-bedroom brick bungalow. This is when I learned about vision. I could see clearly the house and yard, the gardens, a pool and a new truck in the drive.

When the weather broke and spring arrived, I was called for an interview by Proctor and Gamble. Soon afterwards I joined their production facility as a line operator, and it wasn't long before we were financially back on our feet. I began construction on our home, and I also purchased a new truck. Months later I was standing in the driveway of our new home admiring the reality of my vision when my wife drove up in a new Firebird. Fifteen minutes later she was heading down the road to take up with one of my co-workers.

That winter my basement flooded and I had to wade through three feet of water to reach the electrical panel and turn off the power. Life wasn't much fun that winter alone in a damp house. When spring arrived I celebrated by going four-wheel driving with my buddies. On an isolated gravel track, I took the opportunity to show off. I took a final swig of my beer, tossed the can away and promptly lost control, drove over a cliff of rocks and totaled my truck. When the interest rates rose to an all-time high, the bank took my house. I slugged the guy at work who stole my wife, then lost my job.

That was 28 years ago, and things have really improved. Today I enjoy a lifestyle that is the envy of many. My relationship with my spouse, my children and my family is superb. My business provides me with a level of satisfaction that brings a daily smile to my face. My financial situation and health is proof that managing change successfully places me at a level of performance that can only be classified as excellent. I've learned that you can create positive change with vision and

perseverance, and overcome the negative changes that are an
unavoidable part of life. And I still think there's an opportunity to
write a country song about it all.

So you see, change can affect you both negatively and positively. It can
come from sources unknown, out of your control, or it can come from
your own desire to improve your life. Regardless of how, where, who or
what created that change, I can assure you, it is manageable. And in most
cases, the results will leave you better off than you were. I believe the
ability to recognize opportunities from change and the desire to achieve
something better not only saved me, it made me stronger and more
passionate.

Subtle or significant—every moment we are alive we experience change.
Too often, we see change as a problem. However, by managing change—
whatever form it takes—we can produce the result we're looking for, or at
least an improved outcome.

"We cannot become what we want to be by remaining what we are."

Max DePree

Change is necessary to sustain, adapt or improve. If you can't adapt to
change, plan for change, or improve on current practices and situations in
your personal life or your business environment, your chances of achieving
performance excellence in either area is uncertain. Worse yet, you could be
putting yourself or your business at risk.

Henry Ford told potential customers in the early 1900s that they
could have any color Model T they desired, as long as it was black.
Soon after that statement he found himself reacting to change
when people chose to visit the Dodge Brothers showroom where
green and blue vehicles were prominently displayed.

If it's a dinosaur you want to be, don't change. But remember what eventually happened to the dinosaurs. They now fuel our cars.

Why You Need to Manage Change

"In the middle of difficulty lies opportunity."

Albert Einstein

OK, you say, change is inevitable. But why is managing it so important? Let's look at some of the things that could go wrong without a defined process for managing change:

FIRST, you might overlook an opportunity to change proactively. For example, let's say you're an electronics distributor. If you don't assess the way you currently ship products to your customers, you won't know how much it costs and you might never realize that simply practicing a better procedure could reduce the cost per unit.

SECOND, if you *do* recognize the opportunity but fail to manage the change initiative effectively, the transformation cycle may take longer or cost more than expected, or both.

THIRD, the change outcome may not be as good as you hoped, or worse yet, the initiative may fail to achieve the desired results altogether. For example, if you are managing your electronics business "as usual" while a competitor identifies an opportunity to reduce costs and sell the product more cheaply, you could easily lose market share and see your profits drop.

FOURTH, the change process may be costly. If you decide to improve your shipping and receiving method, but you execute those improvements without a defined Change Management Process, the resulting disruption to your existing business and clientele may hurt your overall business rather than improve it and result in cost overruns and project delays.

FIFTH, if the results of your change initiative are less than desirable, it could discourage you from future attempts to change.

Change management is the ability to recognize opportunities for improvement within a problem and take proactive measures to control its outcome. In other words, to identify, recognize, manage and control change so that you get the results you want.

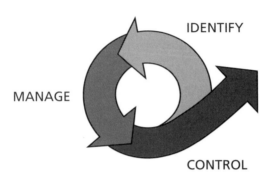

IDENTIFY

MANAGE

CONTROL

Types of Change

Change can be recognized and managed as a proactive initiative, or handled as a reactive response. Understanding these two types of change and their characteristics will help you identify, manage and control any situation. Let's look at both.

Reactive Change

When an unplanned event creates an uncomfortable situation or problematic condition, you're forced to *react* to change. Millions of individuals have had their routines shattered by unexpected change: their own illness or the illness or death of a loved one, loss of a job, divorce, unplanned pregnancy, and so on. Many businesses have unexpectedly had to change when the economy shifts, consumer tastes change, or the competition becomes stiffer. Unfortunately, in many cases, individuals and businesses fail to predict change, plan for it and stay in control.

I recall a situation in the soft drink industry when a particular manufacturer developed a diet soft drink that took the competition by surprise and gained significant market share. It would have been business management suicide for the competition not to react by developing a similar product to regain market share, so all the other soft drink manufacturers were forced to scramble to develop their own diet cola as quickly as possible. A similar situation occurred in the automobile manufacturing industry when the minivan was introduced.

Reacting to change is a risky method of managing change. Although it's sometimes unavoidable, it should never be considered a method of managing change. All it takes to avoid reactive change is to understand that change is not only inevitable, but also necessary to maintain the quality of your life and to grow your business. That's why you need to expect change and plan for it proactively.

Proactive Change

It is much easier to deal with any situation when you expect it and plan for it. That means assessing your situation and then setting a path for success based on pre-determined goals and objectives. The pioneering soft drink manufacturer predicted shifts in consumer tastes and planned a way to take advantage of that change: developing a diet soda.

You can create proactive change in your personal, work or business environment simply by establishing a future vision. If you see yourself retiring at the age of 55 and spending your time woodworking, boating, and traveling, for example, you'll soon realize that to achieve your vision you will have to be proactive. To enjoy retirement, you'll need to be healthy and financially comfortable—and reaching those goals will require taking action now.

My father established a vision of retiring at age 60 and acquiring his pilot's license. He knew that if he were to succeed in achieving this vision, he would not only have save money for his retirement, but also quit smoking and attend to his health as well. The day he took me flying for the first time, I realized how powerful a vision could be in establishing change.

Business management is no different. When a future vision is established and supported by a strategic plan, it sets positive change in motion.

In my own business I have experienced both reactive and proactive change. The lessons I learned from reactive change taught me to pay close attention to the opportunities provided by proactive change. I no longer wait for things to happen in my business. I take measures to create the environment and opportunities I desire. This is easily accomplished by understanding how to identify, manage and control change so I'm prepared for any undesirable conditions that occur.

A number of years ago, when a business contract was not renewed, I found myself sitting on debts with no opportunities for more business. When I finally acquired the work I needed to get back on my feet, I decided that I would be more proactive in managing my business. Big or small, every business is at risk if managers don't learn how to recognize change opportunities and use them to their advantage.

"Difficulties mastered are opportunities won."

Winston Churchill

Dealing with Fear and Resistance to Change

If we make changes to a company's production equipment, such as a production-line lube system, to increase its performance or reliability, we won't encounter any emotional resistance from the equipment. It simply performs in accordance to the new design or modifications. A flip of a switch or turn of a valve, and the change is complete.

The same, however, cannot be said for people. Moving outside of the circle of comfort and familiarity (the status quo) is stressful. Because stress is typically associated with a problem, many people perceive change as the problem, unless they are the ones initiating the change. In that case they see the change as practical and sensible—an opportunity to resolve an existing problem or improve an existing practice.

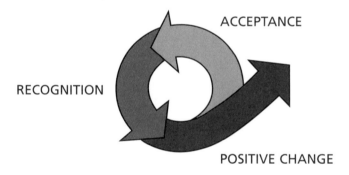

Fear of failure or loss is so strong and so real that I sometimes wonder how I am ever going to succeed with my consulting assignment to assist company employees through the process. I've found that providing support in the form of personal understanding and experience is the most successful approach— reassuring everyone involved that I've been there, done that, and survived and prospered, and they can too.

Successful change management depends on eliminating any fear or resistance and establishing some level of acceptance. To do that, you need to recognize and understand the most common reasons why individuals and businesses fear and resist change:

1. Lack of planning: Instead of anticipating and managing change, surprise catches many individuals and businesses, forcing them into uncomfortable change actions and situations.

2. Being trapped in a comfort zone: In times of disorder, individuals and businesses like to fall back to the status quo because familiar practices produce consistent, expected results.

3. Fear of the unknown: Many people prefer the devil they know to the devil they don't.

4. Poor understanding of the reasons for change: If you're initiating a change, you need to explain the benefits clearly to everyone who will be affected.

5. Poor understanding of the goals and objectives of the change opportunity initiative: If you're initiating a change, you also need to explain the goals and objectives clearly.

6. Fear of failure: Most people are generally not risk takers. They're not sure they'll be able to do things the new way, or they're afraid the new way won't produce better results.

7. Lack of confidence: Individuals or businesses often have no confidence in the person leading the change opportunity initiative.

8. Lack of consultation: People may see better ways to solve the problem, but have no opportunity for input.

9. More effort, same compensation: People often believe change will involve working more without any greater personal rewards.

10. History: If past efforts to create change have not produced the desired results, people won't be as receptive to change.

11. Defensiveness: Individuals may see the proposed change as an attack on their performance.

12. Satisfaction with the status quo: If people are happy with their current co-workers, friends and surroundings, they may see change as a threat.

13. Finally, people resist change simply because it is change.

A Venezuelan friend once told me:

"El que no apuesta ni gana ni pierde."
(Those who do not bet do not lose, but neither do they win.)

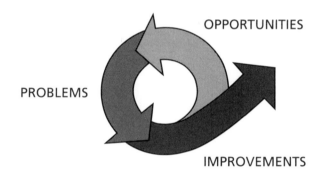

PROBLEMS

OPPORTUNITIES

IMPROVEMENTS

If we could establish an environment where pleasure rather than discomfort was associated with a change to a way of doing something, wouldn't it make sense that success would follow? There are many things you can do to deal with fear and resistance to change:

1. Evaluate each individual's level of receptivity to change, using questionnaires and observations. (You'll find a questionnaire you can use a little later in this chapter.)

2. Identify individuals who are more receptive to change and have them assist with the change opportunity initiative. One of the well-documented laws of organizational behavior is that involvement leads to commitment. Use a high-involvement approach to achieve the high level of commitment that is essential for the success of your change process.

3. Involve individuals who are not receptive to change by partnering them with someone who is more receptive.

4. Educate individuals and businesses on change management concepts.

5. Provide an opportunity for people to see the results you're trying to achieve—such as best practices or industry benchmarks—through training workshops and seminars, benchmarking institutes, site tours, Internet research, networking, trade shows, and reading materials.

6. Involve individuals in comparing how things are currently done— current practices—to the best practices you want to achieve.

7. Clearly communicate the need for change and the goals and objectives of the change opportunity initiative.

8. Encourage everyone to identify opportunities for improvement, and listen to their suggestions seriously.

9. Continually focus on the positive aspects of the change.

10. Establish change management leaders and teams.

11. Involve individuals in the planning phase of the Change Management Process.

12. Involve individuals in the implementation phase of the Change Management Process.

We'll discuss many of these in more detail in the chapters that follow.

Understanding Personality Types

When it comes to supporting people through a process of change, it helps to understand whether someone is an introvert or an extrovert. Neither one is good, bad or better than the other. It simply determines how an individual responds or deals with change situations. Both introverts and extroverts add equal value to a change improvement project if you recognize their emotional comfort level and respond accordingly. Keep in mind that an individual may possess a combination of both qualities, or shift from one to the other depending on the situation. Someone might be an *introvert* when working in a group and an extrovert when working alone, or an *extrovert* at home but an introvert at work.

Introverts can be described as those who shy away from change. They are generally not risk takers. Their nature is to gather all the facts and analyze data before making a decision. They are excellent developers because they quite often enjoy working alone and having control over a situation. Any change initiated by them will have a high success rate.

Extroverts can be described as those who are outgoing and assertive. They are generally risk takers and decisive, making them more comfortable with change initiated by others. They are often admired and respected for their leadership and involvement in progress. This makes them ideal candidates for implementing a Change Management Process.

Providing Motivation

Motivation is a wonderful change initiator, and there are many ways to motivate individuals to change in their personal life or their workplace:

- **MONETARY:** One of the most common methods of motivation is to promise increased financial compensation. Money alone, however, cannot create a desire or passion for change. An individual may simply comply with change to get more money.

- **THREAT:** Threats are dangerous but common motivators that do little to enhance an individual's performance. Again, an individual may simply comply with change to avoid the consequences.

- **RECOGNITION:** This can be a powerful motivator. In continuous small doses, recognition can significantly increase the success of change.

- **TRUST:** Like recognition, trust can significantly enhance acceptance of change and can improve performance.

- **LIFESTYLE AND BENEFITS:** Feeling better, having greater financial freedom, and enjoying the benefits of a good lifestyle can motivate individuals to change. As a business owner or manager, you may wish to promote this opportunity to its fullest potential. Healthy and happy employees typically perform at a level of excellence. For many, this may be as simple as providing financial counseling or training, childcare, health benefits, time out for resting, compensation for cycling to work (which in many cases saves parking costs to the employer), establishing a company fitness center, etc.

During my work assignment in Venezuela, we were encouraged to take a two-hour lunch break that included a siesta. I'm not saying this is practical for all businesses, but it sure motivated me to return to work each afternoon, refreshed, and ready to perform almost as well as I did in the morning.

- **PROMOTION:** The promise of a better position can motivate individuals in a very positive fashion as long as the promise is honored.

- **DESIRE TO SURVIVE:** For individuals who are reacting to changes such as health problems, divorce, job loss, or business losses, the desire to survive can be a powerful motivator.

- **TEAMWORK:** One of the many benefits of establishing a team environment is the motivation and support that each person gives to and receives from fellow team members. It is important, however, to recognize that each member of the team must have the passion and vision to succeed. As well, each team must have leadership—teamwork without management or leadership is a recipe for disaster.

- **RESULTS:** Seeing the results of change can significantly motivate individuals. However, it generally takes some other motivator to begin the change process, because it takes time to begin seeing results.

- **WINNING:** The natural desire of individuals to win can be a powerful motivator. Winning does not necessarily have to be at the cost of another's loss. It can simply be the achievement of a specified objective or goal.

Encouraging Passion

Passion is the most powerful emotion leading to successful change. Unfortunately, passion cannot be transferred; it has to come from within. I am passionate about many things: for example, my spouse and lifestyle, my business and the writing of this book. Anyone with a passion for golf will play it as often as possible. Motivation is not an issue, because the enjoyment of the activity itself is the reward.

While passion cannot be given, it can be introduced. For example, a friend of mine never considered flying an airplane; in fact he had never been in a small plane in his life. Yet at age 39 he was invited to go flying with a friend and found that it was the most exciting experience he had felt in years. He became so passionate about flying; he changed careers and now owns a fly-in fishing business.

Removing Barriers

It's difficult to learn or re-learn a procedure. It takes a lot of work with few results to show for it at first. On a personal level I know from experience that learning to speak Spanish required a lot of effort to achieve the smallest gains. It wasn't until I began to see real improvement in my ability to speak with people that I became more comfortable and more motivated to achieve.

This is where managers have an opportunity to create a learning environment by encouraging and reassuring any employee who is resisting change. Through orientation, training and coaching—all of which are discussed in detail in subsequent chapters—a manager can provide an employee with the time and support required to reduce the learning curve.

As individuals are learning new procedures, the pressure to achieve a certain level of performance or meet deadlines can cause them to resist change. Allow people to be themselves and learn at a pace that is comfortable for them. This does not mean, however, that they shouldn't strive towards measurable goals and objectives; it simply means each individual must have the resources and capacity to achieve those targets.

Evaluating Change Attitudes

How receptive are you to change? How receptive to change are your partner, co-workers or employees? If you or the people around you are going to be involved in a change improvement project, evaluating change attitudes can help you manage the process better. Take a few moments to answer the following questions as honestly as possible.

Once you've completed the questionnaire, follow the scoring instructions at the end.

Change Attitude Questionnaire

1. I have improved one or more areas in my personal life through changes to my relationships, health, or finances.

    a. A great deal
    b. To some degree
    c. More or less
    d. Not really
    e. Didn't have to

2. I have improved one or more areas in my work environment through changes to my attitude, competency, performance, attendance, or input and involvement.

    a. A great deal
    b. To some degree
    c. More or less
    d. Not really
    e. Didn't have to

3. If I quit my job, someone could take my place and carry on with business as usual.

    a. Agree
    b. Somewhat agree
    c. Disagree

4. The older you are, the harder it is to change.

    a. Disagree
    b. Somewhat agree
    c. Agree

5. My age group is:

    a. 15 – 20
    b. 21 – 25
    c. 26 – 35
    d. 36 – 50
    e. 50 +

6. More often than not, change has enhanced my environment.

    a. True
    b. False

7. I experience pleasure when changes make something look or function better.

    a. Agree
    b. Somewhat agree
    c. Disagree

8. I understand the term "Flavor of the Month" is a negative phrase directed towards change initiatives, but I don't let that bother me.

    a. True
    b. False

9. I am usually asked for my input when changes are being made.

    a. Most often
    b. Sometimes
    c. Never

10. I feel I could contribute to the success of a change improvement project if I were asked to.

    a. Strongly agree
    b. Agree
    c. Somewhat agree
    d. Uncertain

11. I have an idea that I would like to patent.

    a. Yes, definitely

    b. Perhaps

    c. No, not really

12. I would like to manage my own business one day.

    a. Yes, definitely

    b. Perhaps

    c. No, not really

13. I look for change opportunities in my personal life and my work or business environment on a regular basis.

    a. Yes

    b. Somewhat

    c. No, not really

14. I like to manage change opportunities.

    a. Yes

    b. Somewhat

    c. No, not really

15. I am creative and enjoy improving existing practices.

    a. Yes

    b. Somewhat

    c. No, not really

16. I believe I am open-minded.

    a. Yes

    b. Somewhat

    c. Could improve

17. I see the value in making changes to the way something is done.

    a. Yes

    b. Somewhat

    c. No, not really

18. Not all current practices need to be changed.

    a. Disagree

    b. Somewhat agree

    c. Agree

19. I have been in my previous position for:

    a. 1 – 5 years

    b. 6 – 10 years

    c. 11 – 20 years

    d. Over 20 years

20. Over my lifetime, I have moved:

    a. Over 5 times

    b. 3 – 4 times

    c. 1 – 2 times

    d. Never

21. It bothers me when a neighbor puts their house up for sale.

    a. No, not really

    b. Somewhat

    c. Yes

22. I have a favorite restaurant that I enjoy, so I seldom venture out to other establishments.

    a. Yes

    b. Somewhat

    c. No, not really

23. I manage my work environment based on clearly defined written guidelines and procedures.

    a. Agree

    b. Somewhat agree

    c. Disagree

24. I know what I would change if I were in charge.

    a. True

    b. False

25. I would like to attend change management training.

    a. Yes

    b. Unsure

    c. No, not really

26. I lose sleep worrying about the effect of change in my personal or work environment.

    a. No

    b. Sometimes

    c. Yes

27. I can think of more than one change that has enhanced my personal life or work environment.

    a. Yes

    b. Somewhat

    c. No, not really

28. I avoid negative co-workers and relationships.

    a. Always

    b. Sometimes

    c. Not an issue

29. Which one of these statements is more effective in communicating with others?

      a. Do you understand?

      b. Do you have anything to add?

      c. That is all you need to know.

      d. None of the above.

30. I have researched the topic of change.

      a. Yes, more than once

      b. Yes, once

      c. No, never

Change Attitude Evaluation Scoring

To determine the results of the evaluation:

FIRST, add up the number of times you chose each letter and enter your totals in the brackets provided. Then multiply each total by the number provided to get your score for each letter.

    a (   ) x 5 = _____

    b (   ) x 2 = _____

    c (   ) x 2 = _____

    d (   ) x 1 = _____

    e (   ) x 1 = _____

SECOND, add your "a" and "b" scores together

    a (   ) + b (   ) = _____

THIRD, add your "c" "d" and "e" scores together

$$c\,(\quad) + d\,(\quad) + e\,(\quad) = \underline{\hspace{3cm}}$$

FOURTH, subtract the total of your "c" "d" and "e" scores from the total of your "a" and "b" scores to determine your final score.

$$\text{a and b }(\quad) - \text{c, d and e }(\quad) = \underline{\hspace{3cm}}$$

Change Attitude Evaluation Results

110 – 150

If your score is between 110 and 150, either you have been involved and shared in the success of a change improvement project, or your personality and view on life help you see change as a positive experience. You accept changing conditions and derive pleasure from change. Your involvement in a change improvement project would contribute significantly to its success.

80 – 109

If your score is between 80 and 109, you most likely recognize that change is a fact of life. If change is going to take place, you would prefer to be involved and have some influence on the outcome. Rather than let change determine what happens to you, you take steps to ensure that you will have some control over change to make it a positive experience.

50 – 79

If your score is between 50 and 79, you most likely recognize that change is a fact of life, but you do not necessarily wish to be involved in it. If other people initiate change, you adapt because you have to. However, your ability to adapt to change is a gift. This characteristic would make you a welcome member of a change improvement team if you were take that small step from acceptance to active involvement.

0 – 49

If your score is between 0 and 49, you generally do not like change. Perhaps you have been in an unchanging environment for many years, or you are at an age where change is difficult to accept. You may not want to be part of a change improvement project because you feel uncomfortable with change and derive no pleasure from creating it. You may be missing opportunities. It is not too late—getting involved in a change improvement project or creating change yourself can enhance your personal and work environment.

Note: *These evaluation results are not based on scientific studies. Instead, they reflect the results I've obtained over many years as a change management consultant. I've found the results from this questionnaire are a good tool for matching people and responsibilities during a change improvement project, as well as with identifying orientation and training requirements.*

A Note about Culture Change

Culture refers to the principles, values and standards within a family, society or organization, which in turn establish customs. These customs, "ways of life" or traditions have generally taken many years to evolve, making any change that much more difficult to achieve. For this reason it is critical that any change opportunity initiative identify and address any cultural issues.

Culture change occurs when individuals and business organizations are faced not only with a change to the way of doing something, but also a change to a way of thinking and acting based on new and unfamiliar customs and standards. This type of change is very difficult to manage and nearly impossible if it's not completely understood.

As I'm writing this book, my wife Toonie and I are living in Venezuela experiencing culture change ourselves. Although grocery shopping and banking were both activities we practiced in Canada on a routine basis, in

Venezuela, we have had to adjust to different customs and standards of language, currency and culture as we tackle these basic necessities. Each time we visit the grocery store, we never know if they are going to have dairy products in stock. Some days they do, other days, nada. This is the accepted culture here. While fruits and vegetables are displayed in similar fashion to our North American stores, they are not washed prior to being displayed. Then there is the bank. Lining up for hours isn't unusual, with gun-toting security soldiers staring at us. These are all cultural differences that we have to learn to accept.

Internal Culture Change

Internal culture change considers the influence of customs and standards from within. For example, children who grew up in a family where poor performance and waste were acceptable would go through culture change if they suddenly had to perform better and reduce waste.

External Culture Change

External culture change considers the influence of customs and standards from society. The same set of procedures could be practiced in two different countries with entirely different results—the difference being the customary approach and attitude towards work and performance. In some societies, a certain level of wasted time and wasted product is acceptable. Therefore, changing a way of doing something may not mean a change in practice, but simply a change in culture.

For example, if I wish to assemble a specific number of automobiles that meet a specific standard of quality, I can't expect to assemble the same number of automobiles in other regions of the world as in North America. What may be essential according to North America culture may be entirely non-essential in other countries.

Culture Change and Training

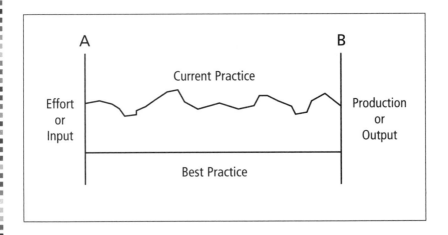

In the illustration above, reducing waste can significantly reduce the amount of effort required to produce a desired result. If we reduce waste by modifying a piece of equipment, we don't need to train or orient that equipment in any way—we just make the change and then monitor its performance.

The same is not true, however, with people. Whenever we change a practice to make it more efficient, the individuals who perform it will experience culture change. That's why training is necessary to help them reach a certain level of comfort in the new standard or custom.

Conclusions

Regardless of whether change is the result of careful planning or an unexpected problem, it *should* be viewed as an opportunity. At one time or another, we're guaranteed to encounter unexpected situations that require us to adapt to change. Believing that all change provides opportunity is a very important first step in successfully managing change.

The I Ching symbol represents "danger and opportunity"—most people see only danger, while few see opportunity. Seeing the risk involved can protect you from mistakes, but you must also learn to uncover the opportunity if you wish to successfully manage change and enhance performance.

"Problems are just opportunities in work clothes."

So let's agree that change is certain, without change we can never reach our full potential as individuals or businesses, and rather than be negatively affected by change, we could look at ways to contribute to the change transition and establish a pleasurable and successful change environment. The following chapters will explain how to do that.

Chapter 1 Checklist: Understanding Change

1 Why Change Is Necessary

☐ I have read and understand Why Change Is Necessary.

2 Why You Need to Manage Change

☐ I have read and understand Why You Need to Manage Change.

Change management refers to: _____

_____

_____

_____

3 Types of Change

☐ I have read and understand Types of Change.

Change is change, however all change should be accepted and

recognized as _____

4 Dealing with Fear and Resistance to Change

☐ I have read and understand Dealing with Fear and Resistance

to Change.

5 Evaluating Change Attitudes

☐ I have read and understand Evaluating Change Attitudes.

☐ I have completed the Change Attitude Evaluation and reviewed the results.

My evaluation score is _____

6 A Note about Culture Change

☐ I have read A Note about Culture Change.

☐ I understand that as individuals we all have varying degrees of principles, beliefs and customs that make us unique in the ability to recognize and accept change.

The key is to determine _____

Chapter 2
Model Overview

The Change Management Process we are about to explore is the key to successful change. Understanding and following this process will guarantee you success in any personal or business change you choose to manage. Whether you're reacting to change you can't avoid or you're proactively initiating change, this process will create the results you're looking for.

All too often, people involved or affected by change don't have a clear understanding of what's happening. They fail to see where they are, where they are going, and when the transformation will be complete. That's a recipe for disappointment.

By following the Change Management Process I've developed, you can apply project management techniques to successfully control the process and reach your goals.

The model consists of four distinct phases, broken down into a total of eight steps. This chapter gives you an overview, while the chapters that follow explain each step in more detail. You'll find the model is easy to memorize and easy to apply, regardless of what kind of change you're trying to manage.

The Change Management Process Model

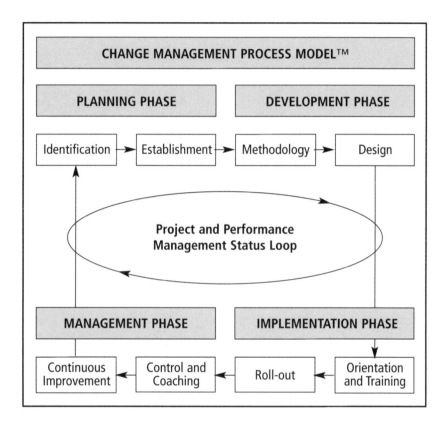

The Change Management Process is a simple but powerful sequence of four phases—planning, development, implementation and management—that can be applied to any kind of change project.

As both the diagram and the list show, each phase is broken down into two steps.

1. Planning Phase
    - Identification
    - Establishment

2. Development Phase
    - Methodology
    - Design

3. Implementation Phase
    - Orientation and Training
    - Roll-out

4. Management Phase
    - Control and Coaching
    - Continuous Improvement

Within each step are a number of tasks that we'll examine in the chapters that follow. If it all looks a little intimidating, don't panic! Each task is very straightforward, and by following the model step by step, you'll be able to create the results you're looking for.

Change Management Process Tasks

1. Planning Phase

   Identification

   a) Establish a steering committee

   b) Create long-range and strategic plans

   c) Perform assessments and gap analysis

   Establishment

   a) Budget and cost control

   b) A change improvement project

   c) A change management team

   d) Responsibility assignment

   e) Project goals and objectives

   f) Key performance targets

   g) A project vision statement

   h) A mission statement

2. Development Phase

   Methodology

   a) Establish key deliverables

   b) Determine objectives

   c) Develop strategies

   - a communication and meeting plan
   - a logistics plan
   - a quality document control plan
   - an orientation and training plan
   - training programs

- a roll-out plan
- a cost control and project status plan
- additional work processes
- job descriptions
- a continuous improvement plan

Design

a) Workflow charts

b) A reference manual

c) Programs, policies, guidelines and procedures

3. Implementation Phase

Orientation and training

a) Conduct orientation and training according to the orientation and training plan

b) Roll-out
   - Roll out the project

4. Management Phase

Control and coaching

a) Update the project status

b) Coach individuals and teams

c) Manage additional work

Continuous improvement

a) Implement the continuous improvement plan

b) Identify learned experiences

c) Assign action items

Timing of the Change Management Phases

The following illustration shows the timing of the various phases and elements of the Change Management Process over the course of a change improvement project. Notice how the management phase spans almost the entire duration of the project. The timing and duration of the other phases and elements are proportionally drawn to give you an idea of how a change improvement project is structured. Of course, the bigger and more complex the project, the longer each phase will last.

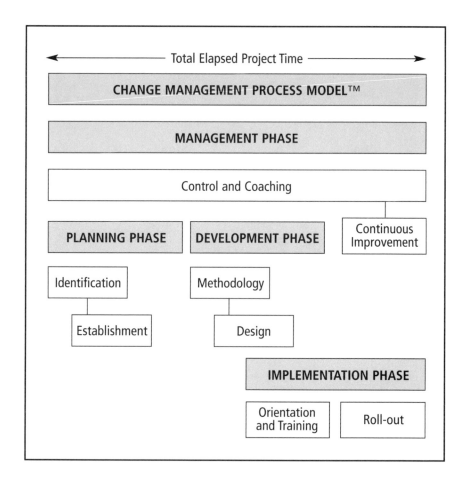

The Planning Phase

Identification

The first phase is identification. This can mean either proactively recognizing the desire or need for change, or reactively recognizing an unexpected, sudden change that must be dealt with. Either way, you need to identify change as an opportunity to adapt or improve.

The keys here are both recognition and acceptance. You need to *recognize* that change must take place, that change is taking place, or that change has taken place, and then *accept* the change, however challenging, for the obvious or hidden opportunities it might provide.

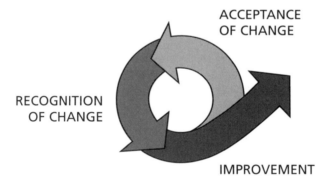

ACCEPTANCE
OF CHANGE

RECOGNITION
OF CHANGE

IMPROVEMENT

Establishment

Next comes establishment. This is about creating a solution in response to the change opportunity you've identified. The solution consists of a project vision, including key performance goals and objectives, followed by a project plan that allows you to control the change so that you can produce the outcome you're looking for.

The Development Phase

Methodology

To develop an effective change project plan, you need to follow a defined methodology. In the development phase, that means *defining* the goals, objectives and strategic tasks, *assigning* responsibility for executing the strategic tasks, and then *controlling* the execution of those tasks.

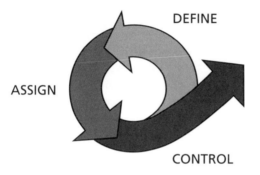

DEFINE

ASSIGN

CONTROL

Design

Design is about creating the necessary workflows, policies, programs, guidelines and procedures that are required to change your current practices—whether they are personal or business practices—so you can attain your project vision and mission. This may sound like a lot of paperwork, but it lays the groundwork for enduring change.

The Implementation Phase

Orientation and Training

All your planning and development work will be wasted if the people involved in putting those plans into action don't know what to do, or aren't convinced it's necessary. Orientation and training must be provided so that anyone affected by the change is prepared to recognize and accept it.

Roll-out

After all that preparation comes roll-out—the moment when you begin conducting your personal or business practices the new way, based on the workflows, programs, policies, guidelines and/or procedures that you've created. The timing and location of roll-out is critical to the success of your change project.

The Management Phase

Control and Coaching

Control is something that happens through the entire change management process, from identification to continuous improvement. It's an essential part of overall project management, using techniques and tools to make sure each aspect of the change project goes according to plan.

Coaching comes towards the end of the project—it follows the orientation and training and makes sure the roll-out element goes smoothly, providing staff with ongoing support and motivation. Coaching during the roll-out element is a critical step that's often-overlooked in many change initiatives.

Without it, implementation of the new order won't be as effective as it could be. Coaching is developed as part of the training plan.

Continuous Improvement

The need for continuous improvement is obvious. Because change is dynamic, and design is never 100 percent perfect, we must continually strive to do and be better. Through continuous improvement, you can use the Change Management Process on an on-going basis to continually improve or adapt.

Chapter 2 Checklist: Model Overview

1 The Change Management Process Model

☐ I have read and understand The Change Management Process Model.

2 The Planning Phase

☐ I have read and understand the definition of the planning phase.

☐ I am now familiar with the two steps that make up the planning phase and am prepared to explore the planning phase in detail in subsequent chapters.

3 The Development Phase

☐ I have read and understand the definition of the development phase.

☐ I am now familiar with the two steps that make up the development phase and am prepared to explore the development phase in detail in subsequent chapters.

4 The Implementation Phase

☐ I have read and understand the definition of the implementation phase.

☐ I am now familiar with the two steps that make up the implementation phase and am prepared to explore the implementation phase in detail in subsequent chapters.

5 The Management Phase

☐ I have read and understand the definition of the management phase.

☐ I am now familiar with the two steps that make up the management phase and am prepared to explore the management phase in detail in subsequent chapters.

Part II   CHANGE MANAGEMENT PROCESS PLANNING PHASE

Chapter 3
Identification

"Any change, even a change for the better, is always accompanied by drawbacks and discomforts."

Arnold Bennett

The first phase of the Change Management Process Model™ is the planning phase, and the first step of the planning phase is identification. So let's start at the beginning. The objective here is to use a variety of methods, techniques and tools to identify opportunities for proactive change.

Sometimes, of course, you have to react to change beyond your control, which means the problem has already been identified for you. But with some assessment and planning, you can turn the perceived problem into an opportunity, regardless of whether it is personal or business related.

The Steering Committee

"Steering Committees should solve problems—not create them."

Rob Thomsett

A steering committee is a group assigned by senior management to oversee a specific change improvement project. Between them, the committee members should represent a range of experience and knowledge regarding the specific project or section of business, and are generally chosen from middle management positions. The amount of time required depends on the size and duration of the project or section of business, and you may need a consultant or interim manager to fill one or more of the positions on the steering committee, or to assist when required.

Quite simply, as the name implies, the role of the steering committee is to steer and guide. Committee members are leaders. They will determine the vision of the improvement initiative, leaving the change management team to determine the best way to reach the end.

There are basically four key roles of the steering committee:

The **FIRST ROLE** encompasses the planning phase steps of identification and establishment. However, before the committee begins investigating improvement opportunities, it may need to allocate money from an existing operating or reserve budget, or request initial funding for the project. Once funding is in place, the committee can assess current processes and practices, identify gaps, and analyze perceived problems to establish a case for change.

In many cases, the steering committee won't be formed until an opportunity for change has been identified. However, there are a lot of advantages to having a committee that looks for change opportunities on an ongoing basis.

If an opportunity does exist, the committee's **SECOND ROLE** is to establish the change improvement project and create a change management team to carry out project tasks.

The **THIRD ROLE** is to establish the goals and objectives, key performance targets, a vision statement, as well as a mission statement, in conjunction with the change management team.

The **FOURTH ROLE** is to oversee the change improvement project and guide the change management team through the development, implementation and management phases to ensure the established goals and objectives are being met. Possibly the most critical role of the steering committee is to oversee and manage the final step—the continuous improvement process.

The committee's time commitment will vary with each phase of the Change Management Process. During the planning phase, the committee generally focuses full time on identification to determine whether an improvement opportunity exists, but after that the workload shifts to part time.

The following diagram illustrates the placement and involvement of the steering committee.

DIAGRAM: Steering Committee Responsibility Breakdown

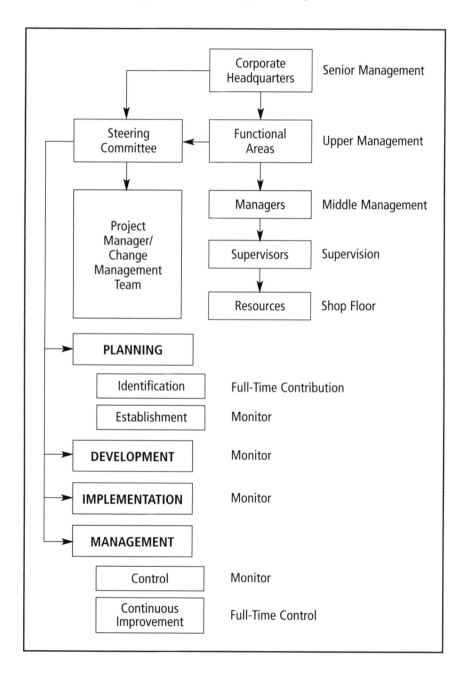

Recognizing Opportunities for Improving through Change

There are all kinds of opportunities for improvement—both personal and business—that ultimately require a change of some sort. Recognizing opportunities is a process that successful individuals and businesses practice on a regular basis. In order to do that, you need to make use of both mental and physical observations.

By mental I am referring to *perceiving* awkward, ineffective, inefficient, harmful or wasteful practices, services, products or outcomes. By physical I am referring to using actual *data* and *management tools* to measure and quantify the way something is currently being done, and comparing it against the way it is done in a best-practice or pacesetter environment.

Change for the sake of changing is seldom successful or profitable, and creating change with unclear objectives or purpose is a recipe for disaster. It's important to identify and assess opportunities for improvement in a way that positively and factually establishes a case for change.

Let's look at how to do that.

What to Change?—Troubleshooting

Usually it's not difficult to identify waste, poor performance or a loss of one type or another. You simply measure the output results of a process, be it a physical process, such as a manufacturing assembly line, or a stakeholder business process, such as customer service or a parts department. The facts will be undisputed in the physical numbers of revenues, profits, stock prices, production and non-conforming product, sales, accidents, and so on. Something is wrong. Something is broken. But what is the root cause?

Until you find out what the problem is, a problem is exactly what you have. You need to troubleshoot it to create the opportunity. It may be tempting to guess or point fingers, but to get to the root of the problem, you need to analyze it. You know the saying: the definition of insane is doing the same thing over and over and expecting different results.

> *In my golf game, I was having problems maintaining any consistency in hitting the ball. Sometimes I lofted the ball, other times I sliced it wildly into another fairway, and sometimes I missed the ball completely. Although each stroke provided an opportunity to improve, I had no idea what to focus on. Through constant, and sometimes annoying, analysis by my mates, we were able to pinpoint the problem: I wasn't keeping my head down until I'd completed the follow-through. I began to practice each stroke with this new method, and after a few games I was consistently hitting the ball with the desired results.*

It's important to pinpoint the underlying source of the problem, or it will just keep recurring. A repairperson can fix an assembly line breakdown, but perhaps the equipment needs to be re-designed, modified, replaced or overhauled to prevent similar breakdowns in the future. Perhaps it was operator error—failure to follow a procedure. Perhaps the operator requires additional training, or perhaps the procedure is invalid.

When a breakdown occurs in a *business process*, the problem is not always identified or recognized immediately. As long as the core business of producing a product or delivering a service, the problem is blurred or invisible until it has a noticeable impact.

For example, an automobile dealership needs someone to order and stock spare parts for the customer service department and keeps the electronic data current. If that doesn't happen properly, there will eventually be problems with servicing customer vehicles.

Once you've recognized a problem with a business process, you need to ask what happened, what broke—just the way you do with equipment failures. Was it poor employee performance, or a problem with the process, software, hardware, or management, or a little bit of each? Perhaps employees require training, the task needs to be better defined, or an opportunity exists to use technology to automatically order parts and reduce the possibility of human element.

The following is a list of items to consider when you're analyzing cause and opportunity:

- Was it human error?

- Was it a workflow process design flaw?

- Was it a policy breakdown?

- Was it a guideline failure?

- Was it a procedural shortcoming?

- Was it a program error?

- Was it a training weakness?

- Was it equipment failure?

- Was it a communication problem?

- Was it a repeated or isolated occurrence?

- Was it a human performance issue?

- Was it a management mistake?

Learned Experiences

One of the best sources of change opportunities comes from learning by doing. *Learned experiences* arise when you observe the result of doing something or creating something a particular way, whether it's how you swing a golf club, ship a container of goods, cut someone's hair, or manufacture a widget. Learned experience is a dynamic and continuous process of looking for waste and for improvement opportunities each and every time something is executed or created.

It doesn't matter whether you're doing something for the first time or the five hundredth time. Either way, analyzing the effort you put in and the result you get can uncover a change improvement opportunity. Look for ways to identify waste within a process or to measure the resulting action, product or service. Eliminating waste provides efficiencies. Analyzing results provides effectiveness.

Learned experiences are associated primarily with the continuous improvement element in the management phase, but they are also relevant in initial planning phase. Refer to Chapter 10, "Continuous Improvement" for additional information on the subject.

Change from the Top Down

Most business change initiatives fail to achieve their desired results simply because of a top-down attitude. Let's break down a company into three basic levels: upper management, middle management, and shop floor staff.

Upper management provides leadership, which is critical to the overall success of a change improvement project. In the absence of leadership, managers have no way of knowing what to manage. Leadership is about effectiveness: the ability to clearly see the project vision, to have eyes forward to navigate obstacles and keep the objectives on course. Leadership is not about ensuring that each task is performed to accomplish an objective aimed at achieving the goal and realizing the vision—this is a quality that must be expected from consultants.

People need to know that someone is leading the way—providing a path of least resistance. They want someone to make them look good if they succeed, and someone to blame if they do not.

Middle management is about efficiency—the ability to manage direct work-related resources to maximize results. Leaders provide direction and point managers in the direction to travel, allowing managers to focus their attention on supporting shop floor staff with instructions and tools.

Shop floor staff, such as line operators, mechanics and front desk clerks, are the people responsible for producing a service or product.

In the discussion that follows, I am making the assumption that upper and middle management are less likely to resist change. That's because upper management is made up of business owners, partners and leaders who create change to improve bottom-line profits. Middle management, I generalize, is made up of managers of financial and human resources. Their desire to change is based on the understanding of bottom-line profits and their overhead position.

This does not mean that upper or middle management never resist change. There are many cases where managers fear the outcome of organizational or market change. However, for the purpose of discussing top-down and bottom-up changes, let's assume that managers are more likely to embrace change than staff on the shop floor.

Business and Work Environment

Change from the top down means that business owners and senior management direct the identification, initiation and management of change. It's the approach used in most business environments today because business owners and senior managers recognize change as an opportunity to improve current conditions—conditions that ultimately affect the bottom line. This does not, however, guarantee success in managing change. Consider the following:

Identify, Initiate and Manage

When upper management establishes unrealistic goals— setting production targets that are too high, for example, or slashing spending—middle management and shop floor staff usually responds with fear and resistance. In addition to their day-to-day activities, managers now have to face unwilling and angry people who weren't consulted. This is not an effective way to implement change from the top down.

Identify and Initiate

When upper management takes on the responsibility of identifying improvement opportunities and initiating the change projects, but leave the management of change to middle management and shop floor staff, the change outcome is *generally* more effective. However, it's still not as effective as it could be.

When upper management limits its responsibility to simply identifying improvement opportunities, while leaving the initiation and management of change to middle management and shop floor staff, the change outcome is <u>often</u> more effective.

I have seen many change opportunity initiatives where improvement opportunities were identified by upper management, developed and implemented by middle management, and imposed upon shop floor staff, only to be met with resistance and failure.

A business *leader* can *effectively* identify improvement opportunities or change necessities. A manager can efficiently initiate and manage the change. Shop floor staff, when involved in the change opportunity initiative, can successfully adapt to the change.

Let's look at the effect that the failure to consult shop floor staff can have:

The owner of an automobile dealership identified an opportunity to improve customer service by establishing a new parts management system. Previously, customers often had to wait overnight for parts to be delivered before their vehicles could be repaired. Management was assigned the responsibility of establishing the new parts management system. Since they didn't have much experience in better practices, they consulted a software vendor that promised a computerized solution. Management purchased the program and had it installed during the evening downtime. Shop floor staff was horrified at having to learn a new program while adjusting their schedules to accommodate the change. It took weeks for them to adapt, and in the end there was no significant improvement to how quickly parts were available.

In this example, there were two serious errors in managing change. First, shop floor staff was not consulted, and second, they didn't get enough orientation so they didn't understand either the owner's vision or the manager's strategies. On top of that, they were forced to go through the effort of learning the new software program.

Now let's look at what happens when you involve shop floor staff in a change improvement project:

Another dealership owner who saw the same improvement opportunity suggested to management that they establish a change improvement project and review the parts management system with shop floor staff. Because shop floor staff was consulted, the project had buy-in from the beginning. At the same time, staff understood the owner's vision and the intent of management to improve the process. As a result, shop floor staff identified a number of opportunities to improve the parts management system based on their experience and the frustrations they'd had with the system in the past. They suggested several solutions that required only a change in procedures and order forms, with a slight modification to their parts tracking and stocking system and their order and delivery process.

DIAGRAM: Change from the Top Down—Business

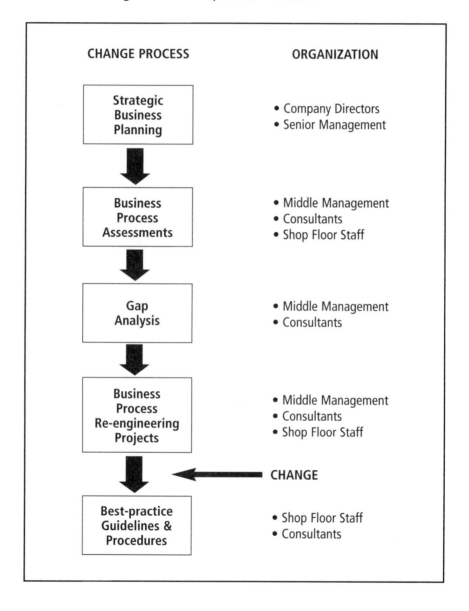

Personal Environment

Personal change management doesn't usually involve a top-down approach, unless personal coaches, trainers, or authority figures are involved. Because these figures are generally certified and more knowledgeable or qualified than you are, you might turn to them to help you with certain kinds of change that demand outside expertise—such as improving your golf game, or boosting your health and well being.

Change from the Bottom Up

Business and Work Environment

Change from the bottom up happens when shop floor staff is the one to identify and initiate change. They might recognize opportunities to improve a work-related activity or situation they are directly involved in, or perhaps they were asked by upper management to get involved in a change improvement project.

Although most change opportunity initiatives are identified, initiated and managed from the top down, they can be successfully identified, initiated and/or managed at any business level. By far the best approach is to share the responsibility for change between upper management, middle management and shop floor staff.

Changes to business practices ultimately mean changes imposed upon individuals. Since we're all human, we're naturally affected emotionally by change. Whether the emotion is positive or negative in nature will depend on our involvement in the change process.

In your personal environment, you identify an opportunity to improve or a need to change, initiate the change and manage the change. You are already familiar with your environment, and you're the one making the decision to change.

That same model can work equally well in a business environment by giving individuals the power to identify an opportunity for change, initiate the change and manage the change successfully.

Most change opportunity initiatives identified by upper and middle management are based on decisions to improve safety, quality, costs or products and services. While these are all valid initiatives, upper and middle management typically know very little about how each of these tasks are carried out. It's difficult to understand the work or the responsibilities of individuals in jobs you haven't done for many years or may have never done. Most of us do, on the other hand, understand our own job responsibilities.

No one knows more about the functional operation of producing assets or the delivery of a service than those individuals performing the operation or delivering the service. Absolutely no one!

The individuals performing the job functions are ideally suited to identify improvement opportunities, initiate change and/or manage a change project. It is far easier to change what you know than what you don't know.

We have no difficulty seeing how ludicrous it is for a group of sales clerks to get together and jointly agree to change the way air traffic is controlled. Directing planes is outside their area of expertise. And yet we have no such difficulty proposing that business executives know how to change the tasks of other individuals whose jobs they have never held, and which they most likely know very little about.

The Path to the Top

If you're serious about encouraging change from the bottom up, you need to establish methods and management tools to provide shop floor staff with a means of initiating change. Nothing is more frustrating for an employee who has a valid and often ingenious idea or plan to change a business practice than to have no means to formally introduce the idea.

Let's look at the example of Tiger Cola (a pseudonym for a soft drink manufacturing company).

Raymond Attwater (also a pseudonym) worked in Tiger Cola's production department. He saw a way to reduce overtime and breakdowns on the production line, so he submitted his idea using the company's Employee Change Opportunity Initiative Form:

EMPLOYEE CHANGE OPPORTUNITY INITIATIVE FORM	
Date: October 21, 2000	**Name:** Raymond Atwater
Department: Production	**Phone:** 7689
Category: Product ☐ Service ☐ Procedure ☑ Other ☐	
Opportunity: The current procedure associated with the mid-stream production change of products to satisfy sales orders is taking too long. Furthermore, the request for product batch orders by the Sales Department is not forecast with enough lead time to allow adequate production line scheduling. The combination of these situations is compounded by the fact that production lines are forgoing their routine scheduled maintenance production outages to make up for lost production time. Overtime and breakdown costs will negatively affect profit per product ratios.	
Change opportunity initiative: As part of a change opportunity initiative I would like to introduce a new procedure to reduce production downtime with regard to mid-stream product changes.	
Action: Initiate ☐ Investigate ☐ Request more information ☐	

Planning for Change

Once you've identified opportunities for change in your personal life or your business environment, you need a plan—a method for making or doing something, or achieving an end.

Whatever your specific goal—whether it's moving to a new house, losing weight, improving project team communication, or reducing injuries on a construction site—you need to know where you are currently, where you want to be and how you intend to get there. Planning enables you to look into the future, visualize goals, establish objectives and develop strategies for obtaining those objectives in pursuit of the end goal. Planning establishes a road map that defines your current position, where you want to go, and how you intend to get there.

Establishing the road map involves two types of planning: *long-range planning*, for personal and business management, and *strategic planning*, primarily for managing expected, or proactive, business change opportunities.

Let's look at both of these.

Long-Range Planning

Long-range planning should not be confused with strategic planning. Long-range planning builds on current goals and practices and proposes modifications for the future. For example, let's say I want to establish a plan for the next two years for my personal relationships, health, and finances. I would identify the current status of each category, and what I want or expect it to be two years from now, based on a clear vision of my end goal.

Usually there is nothing strategic about a long-range plan. It is simply a map outlining the course that an individual or business intends to pursue to reach a specific goal within a specific time frame.

Strategic Planning

In contrast, strategic planning considers changes or anticipated changes in the environment that suggest a more drastic shift from the status quo.

A strategic plan must be based on the company's vision and mission, in contrast to an operational plan, which focuses on shorter-term goals and performance measures. For example, in the process of production planning, supply and demand is identified on short-term weekly or monthly sales, and the type of product to be produced is determined based on established sales and existing accounts. It doesn't take into account future trends or production demands, which may well be very different.

A manager who is planning product developments in the long term may forecast eventually replacing a piece of equipment with a newer model that would increase efficiency and capacity, or perhaps expanding the existing facility. However, when he develops a strategic plan, he analyzes the long-term market trends, alternative opportunities, new technology and other factors. This analysis might determine how much emphasis to put on improving existing products versus developing and marketing new products, and whether it would be wise to increase capital assets, labor resources, or financial capital.

The history of strategic planning begins in the military. According to Webster's *New World Dictionary*, strategy is "the science of planning and directing large-scale military operations, of maneuvering forces into the most advantageous position prior to actual engagement with the enemy." When we apply strategic planning to business management, one element remains key: the aim to achieve competitive advantage.

If you do not know where your business is going, any road will do. Senior business managers are often so preoccupied with immediate issues that they lose sight of their ultimate objectives. That is why a strategic plan is a fundamental necessity. Merely establishing a strategic plan will not ensure success. It will, however, help you improve in a proactive manner that will allow you to anticipate change and ultimately out-maneuver the competition.

Quite simply, strategic planning is the process of identifying the internal strengths and weaknesses of your organization and creating strategies to capitalize on those strengths and overcome the weaknesses. It recognizes that there are also external influences on the organization, so it includes an assessment of both the opportunities and threats. Again, the purpose is to develop strategies that will allow your organization to take advantage of the opportunities while minimizing the threats. It is important to keep in mind the vision, mission, and principal values of the organization while you develop the strategic plan.

How to Develop a Plan

To develop a plan, you need to define, assign and control.

Methodology: Define

Step 1: Begin with a vision—a place you want to be in the future, or a thing you want to have (living in Canada, speaking Spanish, buying a big house in Malibu, having a beer with Julia Roberts, having more money, or successfully completing a project). Record your vision.

Step 2: Next, establish and write down the goals associated with your vision. These are measurable attributes of your vision (live and work in Edmonton, Alberta, Canada by August 2003).

Step 3: Now establish objectives to reach those goals—the measurable milestones or steps that would lead you towards your goals (make a trip to Canada, look for work, learn French).

Step 4: Establish strategies to attain each objective (book a trip with your local travel agent, phone the Canadian consulate for information).

Methodology: Assign

Step 5: Create tasks, and then determine when to do the task (timing), what resources are required, and the duration of the task or milestone. Attach notes if necessary. (For example, the tasks involved in booking a trip are WHERE: local travel agent, WHEN: September 9, 2002, WHO: me, HOW: pay with Visa, WHAT: book for a flight leaving on a Friday and returning two weeks later, book hotels and car rental, exchange money.)

Step 6: Now link these tasks in a logical series, entering the details in a project management program and freezing the schedule.

Methodology: Control

Step 7: Begin executing the plan.

Step 8: Manage the plan by executing tasks and updating the status of the project on a regular basis, perhaps weekly.

Good planning will lead to positive results. The most common mistake in establishing a project is failing to establish a plan. And the most common reason a plan fails is because it lacks one of the components: vision, methodology, goals, objectives, strategies and tasks.

The Role of Consultants

A shepherd is herding his flock in a remote pasture when suddenly a brand new Ford Explorer advances out of a dust cloud towards him. The driver, a young man in a Gigui suit, Gucci shoes, Ray-Ban sunglasses, and a YSL tie leans out of the window and asks the shepherd: "If I tell you how many sheep you have in your flock, will you give me one?"

The shepherd looks at the driver, then at his peacefully grazing flock and calmly responds, "I suppose."

The young man parks his vehicle, takes out his notebook, connects it to a cell phone, surfs to a NASA page on the internet where he calls up a GPS satellite navigation system, scans the area, opens up a database and 60 spreadsheets with complex formulas. Finally he prints out a 150 page report on his hi-tech miniaturized printer, turns to the shepherd and says: "You have exactly 1,586 sheep!"

> *"That is correct, take one of the sheep" says the shepherd. He watches the young man select a sheep and bundle it in his Explorer. Then he says: "If I can tell you exactly what your business is, will you give me back my sheep?"*
>
> *"Okay why not," answers the young man.*
>
> *"Clearly you are a consultant," says the shepherd.*
>
> *"That's correct," says the young man, "but how did you know?"*
>
> *"Easy," answers the shepherd. "You turn up here, although nobody called you. You want to be paid for the answer to a question I already know, and you don't know squat about my business because you just took my dog!!"*

This story is certainly an entertaining perspective on consulting, and like any story it contains a grain of truth. However, most consulting firms would not appear uninvited to compel an individual or business to undertake anything. The level of competence that consultants bring to a change improvement project can contribute significantly to its overall success.

Consulting is about transferring the knowledge obtained through research and experience. Consultants can give you a method of learning, developing and adapting that will increase awareness, performance, profitability and confidence.

However, it is important to recognize that all change depends on the support of the person, or persons, leading the change.

Assuming you have that support in place, when can a consultant be helpful? If your organization doesn't have sufficient qualified resources to manage change, consultants can bring benchmark information and expertise to the table. Obtaining the assistance of an independent consultant, interim manager or consulting firm on a part-time or full-time basis is an option that many companies are taking advantage of.

The consultant's role is to facilitate. There is little value in acquiring the services of someone who identifies, plans, develops and implements change. The resulting change will be effective only while he or she is there to manage the change. No sooner does the consultant depart than things return to their normal state of practice.

An independent consultant, or consulting firm, must provide a service that is built on:

- Principles

- Field experience

- A willingness to transfer knowledge

- Training and orientation skills

- A record of success

Business Process Assessments and Gap Analysis

Many change opportunity initiatives are established using business process assessment and gap analysis. These are ways to identify gaps between current practices and best practices.

What Are Current Practices?

Current practices are the way things are presently done: the procedures, actions, activities or tasks being practiced on a regular basis to produce a product or service. They can be strict or casual, personal or professional.

Professional management consultants measure how effective current practices are by benchmarking them against *best practices* to identify opportunities for improvement. Let's look at these in a little more detail.

What Are Best Practices?

Most companies are not "pacesetters" in every area of business—perfection is hard to achieve! But due to the nature of competition, most try to excel in one field. Maybe they want to be the most admired, the most profitable, or the keenest competitor.

Best practices are documented strategies and practices employed by highly successful companies that provide the most effective return for their resource investment. Consultants identify best practices by gathering and comparing information from a variety of sources, including interviews, surveys, and publications. The time, money, and human effort expended are compared to the potential to generate profit while protecting human life, the environment and capital assets.

Most often the gaps between current practices and best practices indicate opportunities to improve. However, occasionally you may find that a current practice is better than a benchmark best-practice standard. In this case a new benchmark best-practice standard is established.

There are many types of assessment methodologies and tools, some more detailed than others. Here are a few common examples:

- Risk Assessments

- SWOT (Strength, Weaknesses, Opportunities and Threats)

- Performance Assessments

- Business Process Assessments

Personal Change Decisions

The decision whether to change—or what to change—can sometimes be difficult. What if the drawbacks outweigh the benefits?

We all make decisions in our personal life that result in change, and we consciously or unconsciously make these decisions based on the priority of our principal beliefs and values. To help you make those kinds of decisions, I have created a Decision Calculator™ that compares the pros and cons, multiplied by your own priority rating for each one.

Let's look at an example. Perhaps you're wondering whether you should quit your job and start your own local business. You start by identifying the pros and cons. Being closer to home and family is good, but you'll be facing an uncertain income—definitely a con. Once you've listed them all, you then rate the importance of each one on a scale of one to three.

Next, you list up to nine personal priorities—such as health and finances—associated with the pros and cons. The calculator will multiply these priorities against the pro and con values to determine a rating. So if you identify uncertain income as a con and give it an importance of two, the calculator will multiply that against the rating of the relevant priority—in this case, finances.

The calculator adds these ratings on each side and compares them. If the total "pro" rating is higher than the total "con" rating, it supports the idea of starting your own business.

You can use this calculator for any number of personal decisions, from "should I work Saturday," to "should I move closer to the city." Having this information can significantly enhance the outcome of personal change.

For interactive decision-making, please visit my web site at
www.listermanagement.com

DIAGRAM: Example of Change Decision Calculator

Type your question here:		Should I start my own local business as a career change?			
Pro: *Enter a positive number*		Con: *Enter a negative number*		Priority Multiplier	
	Rating		Rating	Health	9
Close to home and family	18	Uncertain income	-4	Relationship	8
Less travel	2	Worry and concern	-9	Family	7
Healthier lifestyle	16	Startup costs	-4	Church	6
		Inexperienced at business	-8	Self	8
				Friendships	4
				Work	3
				Finances	2
Total Pro Rating	36	Total Con Rating	-25	Travel	1
Rating – Pro multipliers		Rating – Con Multipliers		Answer to Consider	
Excellent	3	I can live with it	-1	Negative No.	N
Good	2	Will have some negative effect	-2	Positive No.	Y
Fair	1	Will have negative effect	-3	Zero	?
		Total Decision Rating	11		

Chapter 3 Checklist: Identification

1 The Steering Committee

☐ I have read and understand the Steering Committee.

☐ Yes, I have established a steering committee for the change improvement project.

Or ☐ No, a steering committee isn't appropriate for this change improvement project.

2 Recognizing Opportunities for Improving through Change

☐ I have read and understand Recognizing Opportunities for Improving through Change.

☐ Yes, I have identified a need for change.

Or ☐ No, further analysis must be done to determine change opportunities.

3 Change from the Top Down

☐ I have read and understood Change from the Top Down.

4 Change from the Bottom Up

☐ I have read and understand Change from the Bottom Up.

☐ I have identified a change improvement opportunity as a bottom-up idea.

Or ☐ I have identified a change improvement opportunity as a top-down idea.

5 Planning for Change

☐ I have read and understand Planning for Change.

☐ Yes, I have established a long-range plan.

☐ Yes, I have established a strategic plan.

6 The Role of Consultants

☐ I have read and understand the Role of Consultants.

☐ Yes, I do need consulting assistance.

Or ☐ No, I don't require consulting assistance.

7 Business Process Assessments and Gap Analysis

☐ I have read and understand Business Process Assessments and Gap Analysis.

☐ Yes, I have performed a business process assessment and gap analysis to identify change opportunities.

Or ☐ No, a business process assessment and gap analysis is not applicable.

8 Personal Change Decisions

☐ I have read and understand Personal Change Decisions.

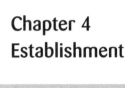

Chapter 4
Establishment

"To change and to change for the better are two different things."

German Proverb

The second step in the planning phase is establishment. Once you've identified a change improvement opportunity and decided to go ahead, you need to assemble resources and establish a project plan outlining the goals, objectives and key performance indicators that make up your change improvement project.

All change, whether personal or business, small or large, requires some degree of resources and planning to control the outcome. In this chapter, we'll look at proactive planning and learn to use the methods and tools you need to establish a change improvement project.

The Change Improvement Project

Moving ahead with a change improvement opportunity means you'll need to set up a change improvement project to manage the steps towards achieving your goal. Keep in mind that whatever form your project takes, it must have a defined deliverable. And, like any project, it will require resources: some combination of money, time, material, research, and human resources, and perhaps tools or equipment as well.

Once you've decided on a change improvement project, give it a name that supports your vision. This is absolutely critical to the recognition and success of your change.

In the case of corporate change, there may be many employees who are not directly involved in the project and may not be aware of its presence. Creating a positive name will draw the attention and interest of employees and customers. Avoid a name that includes "Reengineering"—a word that does not signify good things to come.

> *I worked on a high-profile change improvement project to establish best practices in the manufacturing of packaging equipment, mainly for refrigerated fruits and vegetables. Months into the project, I found that individuals at some levels of the organization were still unaware of its existence or purpose. Subsequently calling the project "Indigo Yield" created universal awareness and interest.*
>
> *"Indigo" represented blue for refrigeration temperature, and "Yield" represented the various crops associated with the business, as well as the ability to minimize waste.*
>
> *Banners, t-shirts, hats and stationery were manufactured and distributed to increase awareness of the current project, and a special logo was developed that became a talisman for all future change improvement projects.*

Establishing awareness of a change improvement project is an important primary step in the Change Management Process. You may want to consider a competition for naming the project.

The Change Management Team

It's up to the steering committee whether to establish a change management team or simply appoint someone to manage the change initiative. This will depend on the size of the project, how critical it is, how complex it is, what resources are available and how tight the timelines are.

The change management team is responsible for making sure the project goals and objectives are met. In a large-scale change improvement project, you may need to establish specialized teams responsible for developing specific administrative plans. These could include meetings and communication plan, a training plan, a roll-out plan and a continuous improvement plan. We'll discuss this later in the chapter.

How to Assemble a Change Management Team

There are a number of things to consider when assembling a change management team—things like expertise, commitment, availability, and representation. There is one critical attribute, however, that you must look for: desire. Ask for volunteers. Develop an organization chart with supporting roles and responsibilities and ask for volunteers to join the team. However, do not promise preferential treatment or bonuses—that will only serve to distance the team members from the individuals who will be affected by the change.

Each member of the team should be well versed in the business and have a high degree of credibility among their peers. They should represent a cross-section of functional areas within the business. This is especially true of change improvement projects that are aimed at developing or reengineering a specific business process that crosses many functional areas—for instance, maintenance, purchasing, and production.

How to Lead and Manage the Change Management Team

How the team is managed will depend on the size of your change project and the staff you have available. Here are a few options to consider:

Champion

Generally a leader, or champion, will be designated to oversee the change management team. The leader will chair meetings, review work assignments and progress, manage costs, act as the team representative to communicate change improvement project information, and work closely with the steering committee. This may be done with the help of a management consultant.

Project Manager

A Project manager may be assigned by the steering committee to oversee, lead and manage the change improvement project if the project size and complexity justify the full-time requirement.

Consultant

If you don't have all the resources and expertise you need in house, hiring a consultant may be a good choice. Consultants can bring a wealth of knowledge and expertise to any project. The key is to find someone with relevant field experience, knowledge and proven change project successes.

Additional Resources

Establishing a change management team from in-house resources will undoubtedly create a void in one or more of the current organizational departments. This void may be temporary or permanent, depending on the scale of the change improvement project. That means finding competent replacements until team members return to normal duties, so make sure you give managers enough time to find a suitable replacement. This is a critical issue because the change management team may well transform into a continuous improvement team after the implementation phase.

Change Management Training

Chapter 7 focuses on how to orient and train everyone who will be affected by the results of the project. Each member of the change management team will be involved in this, so it's essential to train the members of the team and the supporting managers in areas that could include change management skills, communication, project management, training development and presentations.

The Vision Statement

The vision statement reflects the ultimate goal or destination of your journey of change. To make your vision a reality you must establish goals so your vision can be measurable. Equally important, it is an opportunity to express to everyone the value of the change opportunity initiative.

Establishing a vision statement is one of the first items of business for individuals or members of a change management team to address. A well-developed vision statement will provide you with a clear view of the future. A realistic one will inspire everyone involved and pull him along a clearly defined path to a future position.

Create your vision. Set aside a specific block of time to think about who you want to be, what you want to have, and what you want to do in one, two and three years. Think out of the box. You must **DREAM** it before you can **DO** it. Dream big!

Share the Vision

Make it visible. Create a sign with your vision statement. Frame it and put it on the wall in your office. Make it a page in your daily planner, placed at the front where you'll see it often. Tack it to the refrigerator. Place it in the corner of the mirror you look into each morning to shave or put on your makeup. Put it on your screen saver. Do whatever you can to keep it foremost in your thoughts.

Examples of Vision Statements

- To gain "Best in Class" recognition in product quality

- To attain a five-star rating in hotel accommodations

- To achieve a profit/earning ratio of 3 to 1

- To establish a clientele of one thousand satisfied customers

The Mission Statement

Unlike the vision statement, which establishes the ultimate goal of the change improvement project, the mission statement establishes *what* you promise to deliver—either to yourself (if it's a personal change) or your customers. Establishing the mission statement identifies what you intend to do to maintain your established vision.

Like the vision, the mission statement must also be measurable, yet easy to remember.

For example, if the vision of your organization is to *"Establish a clientele of one hundred thousand customers"* with a measurable goal which states *"before the end of the fiscal year,"* the mission may be *"maintain 100 percent line quality and equipment reliability".* How the mission will be accomplished and measured will be covered in subsequent sections and chapters.

Who Should Create the Mission Statement?

Obviously, if you're looking for a mission statement to guide your personal change, you're the best person to create it. You are the only one who knows what you want.

In a business, everyone associated with the service or product must have a role in creating the mission statement. That includes everyone who supplies the service or product, as well as the customers who use it. A mission statement created in isolation will not produce the results you need.

Examples of Mission Statements

- To attend to each customer within 30 seconds of his or her arrival at the pump

- To deliver your product orders on the promised delivery date

- To produce enough quality product to meet the sales department's weekly orders

- To maintain a 99.8 percent production line availability

Project Goals and Objectives

Project goals and objectives should be at the core of the vision statement that you've created for the project—for example, *establish a quality service to provide weekly lawn maintenance to 200 customers before the end of the first business season.*

You should establish goals and objectives as soon as you have identified your change improvement project. They will provide a benchmark that you can use to establish key performance targets. Think of goals as the end result of your ambition. Goals determine the vision, or the last rung on the ladder of project objective achievements. Once the change improvement project is complete, the vision shifts to a mission, and the key deliverables you've established during the methodology step are controlled with key performance indicators.

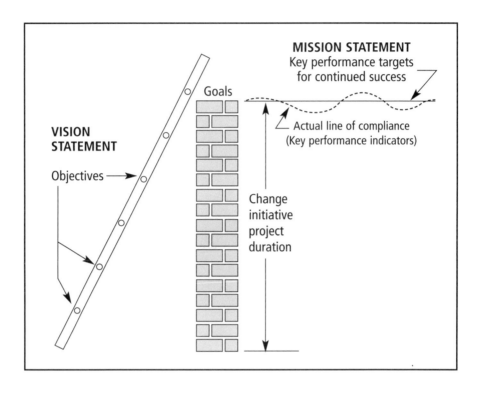

Examples Using Goals and Objectives

Goal: Operate for one year with no lost time incidents

Objectives: • Implement safety program

• Increase the frequency of safety meetings
to one per week

• Enroll all production and maintenance employees
in safety training

• Award safety points monthly that are redeemable
at local merchants

Goal: Reduce cost per unit produced to $12.00
               by February 20xx

Objectives: • Establish a continuous improvement team

               • Enroll employees in continuous improvement
                 training

               • Obtain professional assistance to assess
                 current practices

               • Establish a change improvement project
                 to improve areas of poor practice

Example with Supporting Strategies

Goal: Increase product sales, reduce product cost per unit

Key Deliverables: (Goal, Vision, Dream)

               • Increase product sales by 15% by 3rd quarter 20xx

               • Reduce product cost per unit by 10% by 1st quarter
                 20xx

Objectives: (Steps, Achievements)

               • Increase contacts by 30% – September 20xx

               • Train sales employees – December 20xx

               • Assess production line process and supporting business
                 processes – September 20xx

               • Train production employees in best practices –
                 December 20xx

               • Replace packaging equipment – 1st quarter 20xx

Strategies: • Purchase contact management software

               • Enroll sales personnel in effective sales program

               • Increase the marketing and advertising effort

- Purchase books on effectiveness

- Hire a consultant to help set management priorities and goals

- Hire a consultant to assess the production line process

- Redesign business processes to eliminate unnecessary production down time

- Redesign the organizational structure

Key Performance Indicators and Targets

Key performance *indicators* are established to measure the success of achieving your vision and maintaining your stated mission. A key performance target is set for each indicator A to create a benchmark measurement. This measurement is used to determine performance of ongoing practices aimed at maintaining the goals and objectives you've achieved through a change improvement project.

For example, if my goal is to establish 200 clients within the next two years and I achieve that goal as a result of my change improvement project, 200 clients becomes my benchmark. Now I have to work to maintain an average of 200 or more. It's easy to measure how well I'm meeting the aim of my mission statement: *My mission is to maintain an average of 200 satisfied clients at any one time to maintain a profitable and reliable lawn-care business.*

Key performance targets are also established to measure how well an activity is performed. For example, if my objective is to keep driving my old car for two years before I buy a new one, a key performance target might be to measure the performance of the automobile at pre-determined intervals. I could look at oil consumption, tire wear, brake wear, etc. to determine whether or not my goal—waiting two years to buy a new car— is achievable. Those measurements would also tell me what needs to be done to maintain the objective—keep driving the old car—tire replacement, less travel, more maintenance, overhaul, etc.

The Change Management Plan

The change management plan gives the project some body or content, for lack of a better description.

It's made up of a variety of administrative or support plans and activities developed using the methodology we'll discuss in Chapter 5. The administrative plans are developed to meet the goals and objectives of the project itself.

Administrative Plans

Basically, each phase of the Change Management Process should have a corresponding plan to maintain control and implement change. Once the project is complete, the administrative plans can be filed and used again as templates for future change improvement projects.

A consultant can help you develop these plans. Consider whether any of the following could contribute to your change improvement project:

- Communication and Meeting Plan
- Orientation and Training Plan
- Roll-out Plan
- Continuous Improvement Plan
- Document Control Plan
- Quality Management Plan
- Risk Management Plan
- Data Management Plan
- Cost Control Plan
- Design and Development Plan

Administrative plans will be created during the methodology step of the development phase. You'll find some of best practices for developing these plans in the chapters that follow. *These plans are critical and must be established, developed and merged with the change improvement project.*

The Project Responsibilities Matrix

To create the change management plan and incorporate it into the change improvement project, you need a format for identifying administrative plans and activities, and a method of assigning resources, durations and start/finish times. To accomplish this, use a spreadsheet to create a "project responsibilities matrix."

Put the administrative plans and activities in the leftmost column, and the names of individuals, teams or positions involved in the change improvement project in a row along the top. The concept is to determine what administrative plans are required for the change improvement project and establish the activities required to support the change improvement opportunities identified during the assessments.

The matrix also helps to determine *who* has the responsibility to develop and execute these activities, as well as to assign individuals or teams to the development of the administrative plans. Place an uppercase "R" in the spreadsheet cell that corresponds to the administrative plan or activity and the person who has the primary responsibility for performing that task.

The project manager is responsible for establishing the administrative plans and activities and the assigning tasks, in conjunction with the steering committee.

Once this exercise is completed, you'll have all the necessary parameters to establish the change improvement program and to determine the change management team, or sub-teams. You can transfer the information to a project management tool for schedule development, which we'll discuss later in this chapter.

Steps for Developing the Project Assignment Matrix

EXAMPLE:

Step 1   Use a spreadsheet or sheet of paper to create the following columns:

Planning Phase

- Identification

- Establishment

Development Phase

- Methodology

- Design

Implementation Phase

- Orientation and Training

- Roll-out

Management Phase

- Control and Coaching

- Continuous Improvement

Step 2   Under the "Planning Phase—Identification" column, list the following tasks that need to be established:

- Goals and Objectives

- Budget

- Cost Control Process

- Communication and Meetings Plan

- Project Vision Statement

- Mission Statement

- Business Process Workflow Design

- Key Deliverables

- Key Performance Targets

- Housekeeping Procedures

- Front Desk Procedures

- Maintenance Procedures

- Conference Center Procedures

- Concierge Procedures

Step 3:   Create columns for each person involved in the project.

Step 4:   Now put an "R" in the appropriate cell to note which person is responsible for each task.

Project Assignment Matrix

Project Assignment Matrix **Project Name:** Guests _R_A1	Positions						
Project Description: Establish a "Best in Class" Managment Process	Hotel Manager	Consultant / Facilitator	Front Desk Manager	Maintenance	Housekeeping	Concierge / Bell	Conference Centre
Project Activities							
Establish Goals and Objectives							
Establish Budget							
Establish Cost Control Process							
Establish Communication and Meetings Plan							
Establish Project Vision Statement							
Establish Mission Statement							
Design Business Process Workflow							
Establish Key Deliverables							
Establish Key Performance Targets							
Establish Housekeeping Targets							
Establish Front Desk Procedures							
Establish Maintenance Procedures							
Establish Conference Centre Procedures							
Establish Concierge Procedures							

Project Management

In change management seminars that I led, I asked senior managers and business owners to discuss with their team members what they would do better on their next change improvement project. *"Better project management and control"* was second on the list. It was clear that the lack of management and control was the direct result of poor project management know-how.

Project management is the backbone of change management, but you cannot have effective project management without effective performance management. This means you must be able to measure how well staff contributes to the change improvement project and how well they adapt to the change outcome. To manage means to measure and control—the key is to know *what* to measure and *what* to control.

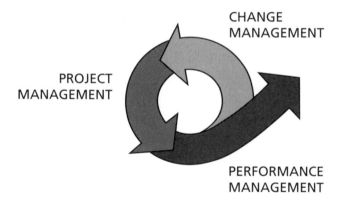

CHANGE
MANAGEMENT

PROJECT
MANAGEMENT

PERFORMANCE
MANAGEMENT

Establishing project goals, objectives and task assignments paves the way for project development. The road map identified through long-range and strategic planning establishes a point of departure (current practice) and a point of arrival (best practice). Driving, not monitoring, is the way to reach the desired destination.

Let's look at the example of losing weight to improve your health and increase your confidence. The first step is to measure your current weight.

This is your departure, and it establishes a baseline against which all further activity is measured. The difference between where you are at any given time compared to your baseline departure is referred to as *variance*.

You must be able to measure variance and make every effort to correct it by changing direction and getting back on the road toward your arrival destination. You need to know where you have been, where you currently stand and where you are going. Monitoring simply looks at what is happening and does not allow for corrections. If you steer too far to the left and take a wrong turn, you will see yourself move away from your goal—your arrival destination.

Driving a change improvement project means establishing the baseline level of current practices, establishing achievable goals and objectives, assigning resources, developing a realistic schedule, and managing and controlling the tasks.

A common mistake in establishing a project is not bothering to create a plan. Many individuals and organizations attempt to develop a project using project management software in the complete absence of goals, objectives and strategies. Tasks, durations and start/finish times and assigning resources are entered without thinking through the reasoning behind it all. A project can be effective only when it is designed to manage a plan. That's why it's critical to follow the methodology of defining, assigning and control.

DEFINE: Establish cost goals (targets) and objectives for achieving the goals. Then determine strategies to achieve the objectives.

ASSIGN: Develop and assign tasks, programs and reports.

CONTROL: Use project management techniques to control the project plan.

Manual Project Management Tools

Manual project management tools are fine for small change projects, especially personal ones. They consist of paper forms that allow you to write down goals, objectives and milestones, and manually record your progress. You'll need to calculate how close you are to meeting your goals and whether you're staying on track. An example of a manual project management tool is shown below.

DIAGRAM: manual project management tool

Project Initiative: Weight Loss		**Date:** March 24
Current STatus: 218 lbs – 38" waist		
Desired Status: 180 lbs – 34" waist		
Goal: Lose 38 lbs and 4" off waistline by August 4		
Reward: Spend $1,000 on new wardrobe		

Objectives and Strategies:
- Drink 6 glasses of water per day
- Walk 2 kilometers per day
- Limit calorie intake to 2600 per day
- Lose 2 lbs per week
- Check progress weekly

Date	Baseline Weight	Actual Weight	Variance/ Notes
March 24	218	218	
March 31	216		
April 7	214		
April 14	212		
April 21	210		
April 28	208		
May 5	206		
May 12	204		
May 19	202		
May 26	200		
June 21	98		
Etc.	Etc.		

Electronic Project Management Tools

It's surprising that, in today's environment of computers and project management software, so few individuals and businesses take advantage of them for managing change improvement projects. There are a number of project management software applications available on the market today.

Steps to Successful Project Development for Project Management and Control

Step 1:   Open your project management software and create a file for your project, identified by the project name.

Step 2:   Create the project responsibilities matrix using the tasks identified in the Change Management Process. Assign each task to a member of the change management team.

Step 3:   Enter the administrative plans and activities into the project file using the change methodology of key deliverables, objectives and strategies. Assign resources based on the results of step 2.

Step 4:   Set up the duration for each activity.

Step 5:   Develop a schedule and establish the start and finish times for each activity by linking tasks or applying mandatory start and finish times.

Step 6:   Identify direct and indirect costs and input these against resources and activities as required.

Step 7:   Establish a reporting structure and create reports.

Step 8:   Generate reports to verify the resource requirements, costs and schedule duration.

Step 9:   Re-schedule activities and resources to optimize the costs, the amount of work allocated to each person, and the duration of the project.

Step 10:   Save a baseline schedule of the project.

Step 11:   Give everyone involved weekly reports identifying the activities they are responsible for executing over the next week.

Step 12:   Each week, update the project tasks, noting which have been completed, what costs were incurred, etc.

Step 13:   Progress and update the project.

Step 14:   Check whether the project is on track and adjust the schedule if necessary.

Step 15:   Reissue weekly work reports as per step 11.

Step 16:   Take corrective action to deal with delays or cost overruns. For example, increase workload, work overtime, increase resources, cancel work, extend project duration, etc.

Step 17:   Assess performances and trends to ensure the project can be successfully completed according to the current schedule, cost and resources.

Step 18:   Let people know how the project is going by distributing progress reports, such as cost, bar chart progress, number of activities completed, etc.

Step 19:   Verify the accuracy of your results. Ask for materials, documents or physical proof that tasks have really been completed. The difference between managing a change improvement project and building a bridge is that progress on the bridge project can easily be quantified by observation. The development of plans, policies, guidelines and procedures is a little more difficult to quantify.

Step 20:   Perform the continuous steps of project management consistently. Once you begin to distribute work status and progress reports on a regular basis, people will expect them regularly. A lack of continued project management will indicate a lack of control or interest in the project itself, not to mention the effects of cost and project duration overruns.

Refer to "Project Status and Updates" in Chapter 9, "Control and Coaching" for additional information.

Budget and Cost Control

When my seminar participants asked their team members what they would do better on their next change improvement project, improved project cost control was also high on the list.

Successful change management shouldn't come at any cost or be allowed to grow out of control. Unfortunately, all too often this is the case, especially with Information Technology projects. Costly or poorly managed projects happen when companies are constantly dealing with reactive, unplanned change; the other reasons are poor definition of the scope of the project and insufficient planning and estimating.

To keep costs under control, you need to establish an investment budget to identify improvement opportunities and allocate sufficient money, time and human resources to your project. This in turn will help you determine the real return on investment—and ultimately decide whether or not to proceed with the change. There is no business sense in proceeding with change that has no real return on investment. We only do this in our personal life, and to some degree in governing territories. If you go ahead with a project, you'll then need to develop a project budget.

It may be more difficult to determine a realistic budget and control costs for change improvement projects that are created as a reactive response to a perceived problem, simply because there may not be time for sufficient planning. Trust me, it's how I learned about reactive change.

Investment Budget

As we've discussed, the first step in a change improvement project is identifying opportunities for change. That's what the investment budget is for. The size of this budget will depend on how much assessment and long-term planning will be required. Consider the following rules of thumb:

- If you know where the opportunity originates, such as breakdowns, short sales, loss of customers, non-conforming product, or accidents, you might not require a formal assessment. However, if you've identified a problem but you don't know how to solve it, you'll need some kind of assessment of best practices or benchmark data.

- If you don't have change expertise in house, consider using the services of a consultant. Make sure that he or she is qualified to assess your particular situation, whether it involves financial performance, sales, human resources, equipment, or marketing.

Change Improvement Project Control Budget

You can create this budget by estimating what direct and indirect resources you'll need for the project and then adding a contingency of 10 percent to the final figure.

To estimate your budget, ask yourself:

What's broken? What is the problem opportunity, or opportunities?

- Programs not working

- Policies not being followed, or delivering poor results

- Human resource performance issues, lack of training, poor procedures, or procedures not being followed

- Poor business processes or related guidelines and procedures

- Equipment breakdown, poor equipment design, or poor operating environment

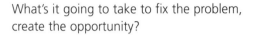

What's it going to take to fix the problem,
create the opportunity?

- Staff

- Consultants

- Equipment

- Engineering

- New design, procedures, processes, equipment

How long will it take to fix? What is the description of the task?
How many people will be needed for how long? What indirect
support will they need?

You'll need to identify each task that will lead to better processes,
programs, physical changes, guidelines, training, policies, and so on.
Decide what resources you'll need—both people and equipment—to
tackle each task, and then calculate the associated cost per unit (hour,
day or fixed price cost).

Now estimate the indirect costs—the cost of supporting resources such
as consultants, hardware, software, office space, transportation,
subsistence, seminars, training, office supplies, etc. These are typically
estimated as a percentage of the overall change improvement project
estimate.

For example, if the total number of staff hours required is 16,000 hours
(10 individuals working 40 hours per week for 40 weeks), at an hourly
rate of $45, the project estimate before fixed price and indirect costs
would be $720,000.

Any fixed price resource or equipment purchases should be added to
this cost. Let's say the project will require a $25,000 software
application and a $120,000 hardware support system, so the total
estimated project cost before indirect costs is $865,000.

At this point we're ready to add indirect costs as a percentage of the overall estimated direct cost of $720,000. The following table illustrates the concept:

DIAGRAM: indirect project costs

Indirect Description	% Cost Low	% Cost High
Office Supplies	2%	4%
Temporary Clerical	1%	3%
Equipment Rental	2%	3%
Consulting	5%	7%
Transportation	2%	4%
Subsistence	3%	5%

By adding the "% Cost Low" of 20% indirect cost adjustments to the direct cost estimate, we get a total of $734,400. We'll add a contingency of 10% to this figure to bring the final control budget total to $807,840.

The percentage of indirect cost adjustments will vary for every change improvement project. It is important, however, to recognize that these costs can be very high and should never be ignored. Many change improvement project budgets have been blown completely out of the water because indirect costs were either not identified or were identified but estimated too low.

The control budget can now be approved, and a method of cost tracking and control can be established.

Cost Tracking and Control

Once the project control budget has been established, you'll need to implement a method of tracking and controlling costs- you must know what you've spent at any point in time and how much money is left.

Budget Status and Control Graph

An important feature in project management software is the ability to track and control costs, much the same way you control project status by tracking task completion. Let's look at some of the elements involved.

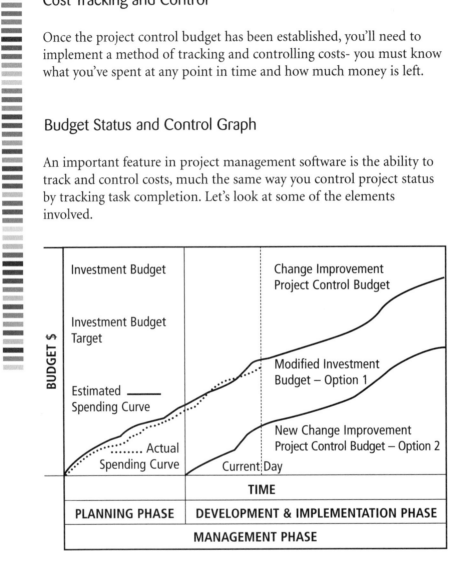

Estimated Cost

The estimated cost is the cost associated with the control budget of your change improvement project. This budget should break down the various project component costs. Managers need to know costs for all aspects of the project, not just the total cost—for example, they may need to know cost by team or group, or cost for transportation, clerical support, office equipment and supplies, etc. Make sure you save a baseline snapshot of the change improvement project so you can track project costs and any variance from your budget.

Earned Cost Values

Earned values are costs associated with completing an estimated task or activity. Whatever the value of time or money (human resource or financial expenditure) estimated against the task or activity, once it is completed it is identified as earned. Let's look at an example:

I estimate it's going to take me 8 hours to replace the brakes on my car: 2 hours for each wheel. When the job is 50% completed, I've earned 4 hours: half of 8. However, in reality I may have run into a snag on the second wheel that takes an extra hour. So although it's taken me 5 hours to do 2 wheels, I'm still only 50% complete, and I've only earned 4 hours.

Actual Cost Values

As tasks are executed and completed, the costs associated with them are realized. Record the actual labor hours, materials used, services, etc. on a specified time basis, such as daily, weekly, or monthly. Now you can compare the actual cost values to the estimated cost values to provide cost status compliance. This will give the change management team the information it needs to take any corrective action required, as well as forecast and analyze spending habits.

Communication and Meetings

When the corporate managers in my seminars asked their team members what they would improve on their next change project, *"communicate better"* was first on the list. Communication is one of the most important and most valuable skills.

It not only provides information, it also establishes a method for interacting and problem solving at a one-to-one, one-to-many, or, many-to-many level. It is important to establish and use effective lines of communication between everyone involved in the change project, from shop floor staff, to managers, suppliers, buyers and shareholders.

In large facilities, many staff can be completely unaware of the change improvement projects currently underway, let alone aware of why the change was necessary. Companies employ individuals for one reason, and one reason only: to perform a function that cannot otherwise be performed by a machine to deliver a desired result, so why is it that companies fail to pass on information that these individuals need to perform the functions they're hired for?

In a case that I observed, the maintenance department of a large oil production facility established a change improvement project to enhance equipment reliability. However, the operations department was completely unaware of the change initiative. Since the operations staff is a vital part of equipment management, they were astounded to learn that maintenance were creating work schedules and requesting equipment shutdowns to perform overhauls on vital equipment. The implementation of this change improvement project was doomed to fail because it didn't involve the affected shop floor staff or provide an orientation that outlined the plan.

Communication Methods

Communicating your message and receiving feedback are critical throughout the project. The method you choose at any particular time will depend on how many people you're trying to reach and what the message is. Here are a few options:

One to One

Informal discussion between two people—whether it's face-to-face or via telephone or email—is a good choice for questioning, directing or informing.

Meetings

Meetings are essential communication tools. For some the very mention of the word "meeting" is enough to send them running in the opposite direction. Meetings can be unproductive, as anyone who attends them on a regular basis will agree; that's often due to a lack of knowledge and effort. People must be trained in how to manage effective meetings. Consider the following guidelines:

- **FIRST**, reserve meetings for situations where no other communication method (face-to-face, email, telephone, fax, etc.) can be used effectively.

- **SECOND**, establish agendas for each meeting. Detail the issues to be addressed and the time allowed for each topic. A four-column format is best: one column each for the issue to be addressed, the objective to be achieved, the process of dealing with each item (such as tasks assignment, brainstorming), and the time allowed for each topic.

- **THIRD**, assign a facilitator to keep the meeting on topic. Assign someone else to take minutes.

- **FOURTH**, begin the meeting on time. Close the door and do not make exceptions for tardiness (planes don't wait; neither should meetings).

- **FIFTH**, ask everyone to turn off his or her cell phones and pagers during the meeting.

- **SIXTH**, arrange the end of the meeting to coincide with lunch or quitting time. No one wants to drag a meeting out and miss either one.

- **SEVENTH**, summarize the results at the end of each meeting and assign action plans and responsibilities. If someone leaves the meeting with no action or responsibility, ask yourself why they were there.

- **EIGHTH**, distribute meeting minutes as promptly as possible.

In addition, think about what form your meeting will take:

Use *orientation meetings* to let people who aren't directly involved in the change improvement project know what it's all about. These meetings, sometimes referred to as "Town Hall Meetings," are a chance to familiarize everyone with the change opportunity initiative and allow them to inquire or express opinions. Choose a location that's big enough, and schedule an hour or two to convey your message and get feedback.

Regularly schedule *project status and update meetings*. The principal leader or consultant overseeing the change management team should chair these meetings.

Use *discussion meetings* to provide an opportunity for individuals who need information relating to one or more functional areas of the Change Management Process to meet with members of the associated department.

Bulletin Boards

The change management team must be able to communicate their work to the entire organization. Bulletin boards are a good choice. Locate them strategically where everyone can see them. Use them to post regular project status updates, the vision statement, the mission statement, contact names and numbers for feedback, notices of upcoming training sessions, and invitations to open-house meetings. Also let people know where they can get additional information, such as the corporate intranet.

Newsletters and Corporate Intranet

Employees are used to reading about corporate business through company newsletters. These newsletters provide an excellent opportunity to introduce change, provide project updates, and solicit new ideas, feedback and employee involvement.

Promotional Items

Consider using promotional items such as hats and t-shirts to introduce change. It's a time-tested method to raise awareness, and one that you can use at any time during the project.

What to Communicate

Communicate the Vision of the Project

Chances are, everyone who will be affected by your change opportunity initiative is going to share their opinions about it with their co-workers. If you want those conversations around the water cooler to be positive ones, make sure that everyone understands the opportunity, the process of taking advantage of it, and the impact it will have.

Communicate Project Status

Keeping everyone aware of the project status is one of the most important communication requirements of the change initiative. Tell them what you want to achieve, what's been achieved, and what's on the horizon.

Communicate the Purpose

A vision statement is not always sufficient for communicating the purpose of change. If that's the case, make sure that the purpose is clear to everyone, whether they are affected or not. People need to know. Organizations cannot afford to ignore their members, employees, shareholders or customers. The more people know about the purpose of the change, the more they will be willing to accept it.

As I write this section I am watching the stock price of a company I am confident is supplying a much-needed and high-quality product. Three months ago trading was halted for a change in Directors and, I suspect, a change in strategy. I am concerned about my stock because I have not read any news or had any update about what is happening. I would like to think positive things are happening, but would feel much better if my email in-box contained a message that gave me some insight.

Don't let the rumor mill communicate the purpose.

Chapter 4– Checklist: Establishment

1 The Change Improvement Project

☐ I have read and understand The Change Improvement Project.

☐ Yes, I have identified a change improvement project.

☐ The project name is:_____

2 The Change Management Team

☐ I have read and understand The Change Management Team.

☐ Yes, I have established a change management team for our change improvement project.

Or ☐ No, my change improvement project does not require a change management team.

3 Vision Statement

☐ I have read and understand The Vision Statement.

☐ Yes, I have established a vision statement for the change improvement project.

4 Mission Statement

☐ I have read and understand The Mission Statement.

☐ Yes, I have established a mission statement to guide the change improvement project.

5 Project Goals and Objectives

☐ I have read and understand Project Goals and Objectives.

☐ Yes, I have established the goals and objectives for the change improvement project.

6 Key Performance Indicators and Targets

☐ I have read and understand Key Performance Indicators and Targets.

☐ Yes, I have established key performance targets for the change improvement project.

7 The Change Management Plan

☐ I have read and understand The Change Management Plan.

☐ Yes, I have established a change management plan for the change improvement project.

☐ Yes, I am establishing the following administrative plans to assist with the implementation of this change improvement project:

☐ Training plan

☐ Implementation plan

☐ Logistics plan

☐ Communication and meetings plan

☐ Continuous improvement plan

☐ Project management plan

☐ Yes, I have used the methodology of "define, assign and control" to establish the administrative plans.

8 The Project Responsibilities Matrix

☐ I have read and understand The Project Responsibilities Matrix.

☐ Yes, I have established a project responsibilities matrix.

☐ Yes, I have assigned individuals and/or teams to each item on the project responsibilities matrix.

9 Project Management

☐ I have read and understand Project Management.

☐ Yes, I have established a project.

☐ Yes, I'm using project management software.

Or ☐ Yes, I'm using manual project management tools.

☐ Yes, I have had training in project management techniques and software navigation.

Or ☐ No, this isn't applicable.

☐ Yes, I have assigned the start, finish and duration dates to the project.

☐ Yes, I have assigned the resources to each task on the project as per the project responsibilities matrix.

10 Budget and Cost Control

☐ I have read and understand Budget and Cost Control.

☐ Yes, I have established a budget and cost control process for the change improvement project.

11 Communication and Meetings

☐ I have read and understand Communication and Meetings.

☐ Yes, I have established a communication and meetings plan for the change improvement project.

Chapter 5
Methodology

"Every really new idea looks crazy at first."

Alfred North Whitehead

The second phase of the Change Management Process Model™ is the development phase. It begins with methodology—defining key deliverables, defining objectives and establishing strategies for change.

If you're embarking on personal change, this may simply mean modifying an existing program, such as a weight loss or exercise program. Business change, on the other hand, may require the development of the many new processes, policies, guidelines, procedures and programs that you determined in the establishment step of the planning phase.

Methodology Defined

Methodology is the most important step in the entire Change Management Process. It's a systematic approach to doing something so that you obtain consistent and valuable results. To develop processes, policies, guidelines, procedures and programs, as well as the administrative plans to support your change improvement project, you need a systematic method.

In the beginning you may wonder what methodology has to do with change management. I know I did, when I first began asking how it would be possible to establish a process to guarantee successful change.

If we think in terms of define, assign and control, it's easier to see that defining goals, objectives and strategies is a planning issue, while assigning responsibility to perform the tasks associated with those strategies is a development issue. Controlling falls under implementation and project management. Most change initiative projects fail to achieve their intended purpose because they don't have a defined methodology, or because the people involved don't understand it.

As we discussed in the last chapter, a change management plan incorporates the key deliverables, objectives and strategies for all the business units and functional areas involved. For example, when a hotel changes its policies or procedures in housekeeping, it may also need to change its policies or procedures in maintenance, reception, accounting, and food services, because all of these areas affect housekeeping.

The project responsibilities matrix you've developed should assign the responsibility for developing the new policies, guidelines or procedures to an individual or team, who should use the change management methodology to do the job.

In addition, you'll need to develop administrative plans—such as safety, communication, training, continuous improvement, administration, transportation and reservations—to support the change improvement project. These too will utilize the change management methodology. Once these individual plans are established, you can combine them to create an overall change management project plan and plug them into the project schedule so that you can measure status-variance and performance. Executing a series of small changes together will result in a successful large change.

Remember that your methodology depends on the goals and objectives of the project itself: what you expect to accomplish (goals and objectives) and how you expect to accomplish them (strategies).

"What we wish may not come true, but what we visualize we can accomplish."

E.J.Lister

Let's consider the following example to understand just how important methodology is in the process of managing change.

VISION:

A successful business with many customers, increased equipment reliability, strong cash flow, etc.

PROJECT GOAL:

Reduce the product cost/unit and increase equipment reliability to 98 percent before year-end. To meet these goals and to continue to enjoy the positive results once the goals have been met, new policies and procedures must be designed and developed. These will include a workflow process, operational and maintenance procedures, production policies, safety plans, training plans, a production plan and a continuous improvement plan.

METHODOLOGY:

Develop and design new operating procedures

Key Deliverables (what the new procedures must deliver to assist in achieving the project goals)

- Effectiveness—they must produce value-added results, where the improvement in quantity or quality is directly attributable to the operational procedures

- Easy-to-follow steps that reduce the amount of effort required by the operators

- Ability to record the status of each step (checklist)

Objectives (what steps to consider when developing and designing the procedures to achieve the key deliverables)

- Develop a standard template

- Research industry best practices

- Use standard language codes

Strategies (what will be done to create the procedure—who, when, how, where, approval, testing, reviewing, etc.)

- Assign operators to develop the procedures during production line downtime

- Enlist consulting services to establish an in-house training session in production best practices

- Assign management supervisors to review each procedure as it is developed

- Test and approve each procedure on Production Line One before they are implemented

- Ask management to develop a feedback form for continuous improvement before the implementation phase

- Incorporate new procedures into the Operational Training Manuals following review, testing and approval

Establish Key Deliverables

Establishing key deliverables is simply a method of identifying what results you're looking for. What do you expect this policy, guideline, procedure or program to deliver at the end of the day? Key deliverables should be itemized, written and achievable.

For example, if the housekeeping department of a major hotel was reengineering its procedures, the key deliverables might be identified as the following:

- Rooms ready in time for earlier check-in

- Zero re-work requested by hotel guests

- Longer lasting linens

- Just-on-time delivery of clean linen and towels by a dedicated team to allow chambermaids to perform their work more efficiently and keep hallways clear of carts

- More efficient bathroom preparation

- Less cleaning noise and equipment in the hallways during peak check-in hours

- More repeat guests, thanks to good housekeeping

Once you've established key deliverables, you can then establish objectives that identify how the deliverables will be achieved. The number of objectives will depend on the number and complexity of the key deliverables and desired outcome. For example, the hotel housekeeping department's objectives might be:

- Encourage guests to re-use towels and linens if they stay for more than one night

- Make routine training a part of the housekeeping policy

- Establish a room preparation delivery and pick-up team

- Buy smaller, easier-to-use hallway carts

- Purchase communication devices for the just-on-time room preparation and pick-up team, coordinated through the check-out desk

- Put the responsibility for zero re-work on the individual doing the work and establish an incentive-based pay rate—number of rooms times preparation time minus re-work (subject to inspection), with additional incentives for positive comments from guests

Determine Strategies

Strategies are how you execute your objectives in a sequential and timely manner. They must be well thought out, keeping the big picture in mind.

Your change improvement project will probably include a number of sub-projects that are developed independently. However, each one of these sub-projects and the objectives and strategies that go with them must be implemented in a well-scheduled and strategic manner through a comprehensive change management plan.

The first step in determining your strategies is to prioritize your objectives. To return to our hotel housekeeping example, priority 1 might be to establish routine training as part of the housekeeping policy, while priority 2 is to establish a room preparation delivery and pick-up team.

The next step is to establish a strategy for accomplishing each objective. So to establish routine training as part of the housekeeping policy, the hotel's strategy might be:

- Contact local training centers to inquire whether housekeeping training programs are available

- Investigate whether the hotel's head office has any training programs available for housekeeping

- Search the Internet for benchmark best practices on hotel housekeeping

- Design a training program using the most experienced and knowledgeable housekeeping staff member

- Establish housekeeping certification and re-examination criteria

Strategies must be supported by tasks. Decide who will be responsible for executing each one then enter the start, finish and duration times of each task in your project management software program, so you can schedule and control them.

DIAGRAM: Change Management Process Model

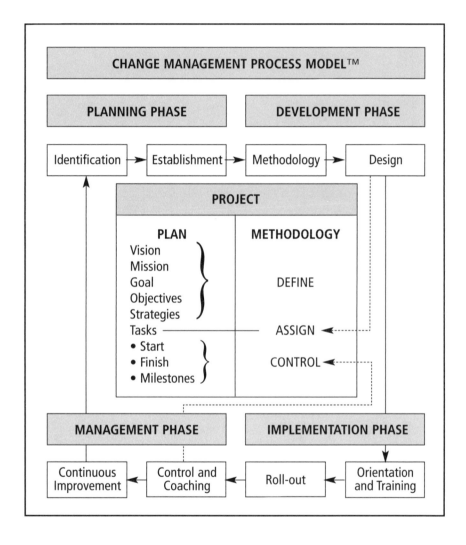

Chapter 5 Checklist: Methodology

1 Methodology Defined

☐ I have read and understand Methodology Defined.

2 Establish Key Deliverables

☐ I have read and understand Establish Key Deliverables.

☐ Yes, I have established key deliverables for the development of processes, policies, guidelines, procedures and programs, as identified in the Project Responsibilities Matrix and Project Schedule from Chapter 4.

3 Determine Strategies

☐ I have read and understand Determine Strategies.

☐ Yes, I have determined strategies for executing and managing each objective and incorporated them into my plan.

Chapter 6
Design

"The important thing is to never stop questioning."

Albert Einstein

The second step in the development phase is design. Once you've developed the key deliverables, objectives and strategies using the methodology from Chapter 5, you can begin designing policies, processes, guidelines, procedures and programs.

Workflow and Process Mapping

Workflow refers to the identification and management of work-related events and activities—all the steps that take place between the supply of raw materials and the delivery of a service or product. You can illustrate workflow with a flowchart, a process often referred to as business process mapping.

Creating a roadmap that illustrates the sequence of events and activities to be accomplished gives you a clear picture of how information and materials flow between the supplier and the customer. It also provides the foundation for the procedures and guidelines that support each event or activity, and creates a tool for tracking the status of tasks. It can be used to measure the time it takes for tasks to be performed, from the time information or materials are supplied until the final goods or services are delivered. Barriers and poorly performing procedures can easily be pinpointed within that workflow.

How to Create a Workflow

Developing the workflow can be considered both an *effective* and *efficient* way of doing business. This means determining not only the right things to do, but also the best way to do them. But remember, no matter how efficient the practice, if the effort and expense don't produce the result you're looking for, you've merely spent time learning an expensive lesson.

When you're designing a workflow, make sure you follow the standard flowchart symbols and related functions. There are a number of software applications today such as Microsoft® Word and PowerPoint® that include appropriate symbols. Using software applications developed specifically for flowchart design and process mapping is advantageous because it saves time.

Whichever choice you make, you must be consistent in using the various flowchart symbols. The ISO9004.4 standard shows just four symbols: start/end, activity, decision and flow line. With these symbols, you can represent any simple process quite clearly. While some flowchart design programs offer you a lot more than four symbols, remember that too many can create confusion and misunderstanding.

Checking Workflow Validity

The flowchart represents a business process. It must not only make sense, it must also be effective and free of bottlenecks. Unfortunately, most computer systems allow you to draw almost anything anywhere, connected to anything. This may be fine when you are illustrating a concept, but not when you're illustrating a business process.

The rules of flowcharting are fairly simple:

- Any assignment must have a task, a subtask, a decision, a start, or an end before it. Likewise it must have a task, a subtask, a decision, a start, or an end after it.

- Flowcharts cannot have endless loops.

The "rules" simply describe the natural way of doing things; for example, one step always follows another. These rules should be built into the computer to ensure that the flowchart is logically correct and to prevent you from carrying out "illegal" operations (or at least to advise against them). The benefits are tremendous; guaranteeing that each flowchart you create is not only correct but also consistent with all the other ones. Consistency and accuracy are what quality ISO standards are all about!

DIAGRAM: Flowchart of Events

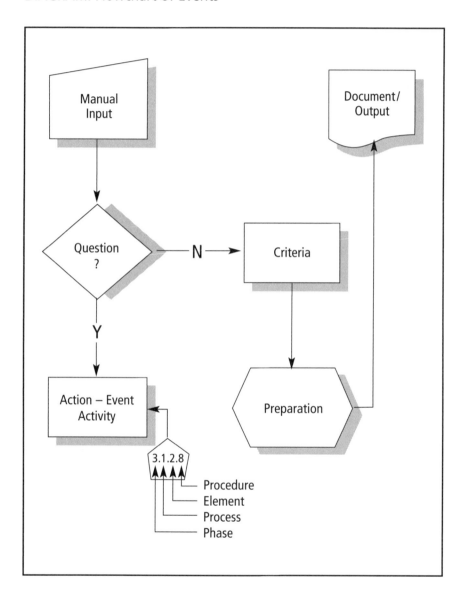

The preceeding flowchart could be used to determine if a request for funding is approved. For example, the Manual Input in the upper left would represent the written request. Beneath it, the Question is, "Is it less than $5000.00?" If the answer is yes, the final action means "provide funding." If the answer is no, the next step is to gather more information (criteria). Once that's done, a formal purchase request is created (preparation), and then printed and filed (document/output) for subsequent approval.

When you're designing a workflow, always begin with the end result in mind such as satisfactory delivery of a product or service. This ensures your workflow will produce the right product or service for the right reason.

Principles, Policies, Guidelines, Procedures, Practices and Programs

Companies do not own people; people come and go. As they do, they bring and take away with them their own way of doing something. However, the company owns the principles, policies, guidelines, procedures and programs by which people are guided.

What we practice makes us perfect. And what we practice most is procedures. To be the best, we need to practice good procedures. This is true for everything from golfing to manufacturing goods and supplying services.

In any business, employees come and go, and physical equipment, computer hardware and software are continually being replaced or upgraded. By establishing consistent guidelines and procedures, businesses can go on uninterrupted and unaffected, regardless of whether people or equipment assets are added or replaced.

Understanding change requires an understanding of principles, policies, guidelines, procedures and practices. Throughout the change process you'll need to evaluate, establish or modify one or more of these. That's why it is important to understand the characteristics of each.

Principles

Principles are the ethical and moral guidelines that determine how individuals and businesses conduct themselves. They determine what actions you take when you're faced with problems, opportunities or options. Although businesses establish guiding principles, the business itself is not a living, breathing entity—it's individuals who ultimately accept the responsibility of making business decisions based on their personal principles.

Your principles are established as moral guidelines from the day you are born, influenced by your parents, teachers, peers, governing bodies and religion. Your principles are based on what you see, hear and experience.

Of course, society has established generally accepted principles of right and wrong, but even so, someone else may not necessarily see what one person considers good that way.

Policies

Policies can best be described as rules for conduct—written or unwritten—that help to maintain order. I believe the following story illustrates the opportunity for policy change in business today.

Start with a cage containing five monkeys. Inside the cage, hang a banana on a string and place a set of stairs under it. Before long, a monkey will go to the stairs and start to climb towards the banana. As soon as it touches the stairs, spray all of the other monkeys with cold water. When another monkey makes an attempt, do the same thing—spray all the other monkeys with cold water. Pretty soon, whenever a monkey tries to climb the stairs, the other monkeys will try to prevent it.

Now, put away the cold water. Remove one monkey from the cage and replace it with a new one. The new monkey sees the banana and wants to climb the stairs. To its surprise and horror, all of the other monkeys attack it. After another attempt and attack, it knows that if it tries to climb the stairs, it will be assaulted.

Next, remove another of the original five monkeys and replace it with a new one. The newcomer goes to the stairs and is attacked. The previous newcomer takes part in the punishment with enthusiasm! Likewise, replace a third original monkey, then a fourth, then a fifth. Every time the newest monkey takes to the stairs, it is attacked. Most of the monkeys that are beating it have no idea why they were not permitted to climb the stairs or why they are participating in the beating of the newest monkey. After all the original monkeys are replaced, none of the remaining monkeys has ever been sprayed with cold water.

Nevertheless, no monkey ever again approaches the stairs to try for the banana. Why not? Because as far as they know that's the way it's always been done around here.

And that, my friends, is how company policy begins.

Guidelines and Procedures

Although guidelines and procedures are often used in the same context, they are not the same. Guidelines "suggest," while procedures "state." Guidelines are a set of general rules or parameters that help you perform a task. For example, most automobile manufactures suggest you replace your motor oil and change your filter every three or four months or 4500 to 5000 miles, regardless of the make or model. These are guidelines. When you do change the motor oil and filter, a more specific set of rules applies. These rules are referred to as procedures: step-by-step instructions specifying such things as the type and amount of oil, type of filter and methods of draining and filling. Procedures are more stringent and designed for a specific purpose.

The success of procedures can be measured by how well they contribute to the overall objective. Procedures may be formal or informal. Procedures for disarming a bomb would be more formal than procedures associated with mixing a cocktail or baking a cake.

Let's look at an example: one company's guideline for controlling expenditures.

Header

Department: *Production*	**Date:** *02/02/02*
Manual Reference No: *Y-333*	**Prodedure Reference** *6.2-A*
Revision No: *2*	**Page No:** *1 of 3*
Guideline: *Identification of a Need for Expenditure*	

Body

Policy: The following guideline provides a method for identifying and approving large expenditures. It guards against unnecessary expenses, which can reduce earnings, profits and fiscal control.

Guideline: A Department Head according to the following procedure must approve any purchase over $5,000.00.

Procedure: Expenditure Approval

- The employee who wants to purchase a good or service must create a Request for Expenditure in the company management software, complete all the required fields, and click on the submit button.

- Every Department Head will review the Request for Expenditure records on a daily basis.

- The Department Head can request additional information or estimates if required.

- If the Department Head approves the request, a Purchase Order will be prepared or the Work Order.

- The Planning Department will review each Work Order on a daily basis for service procurement and scheduling.

- The Purchasing Department will review each Purchase Order and associated line items daily and procure the materials or products as identified.

- The associated Department Head will complete each transaction on a daily basis.

Attachments: See Attachment 6.2-AA - Need for Expenditure Form and Instructions.

Practices

What we live, we learn.

What we learn, we practice.

What we practice, we become.

And, what we become has consequences.

Ernest Larson—"The Essence of Formation"

Practices are the actions associated with performing an activity, task or procedure. The more we practice, the better the result. Ideally, we will continually improve and establish consistent results on a best-practice or pacesetter level.

Let's look at an example of principles, policies, guidelines and procedures in action.

Last Saturday I got up early to take my children to the park to play soccer as I promised them the night before. After lunch, I changed the oil in my car and then spent the rest of the afternoon helping my wife prepare dinner for our guests.

In this scenario my principles support my personal priorities of health, relationships and finances: to exercise, play with the children, maintain my vehicle and spend quality time with my spouse. The manufacturer of my vehicle provided a guideline for how often to change the oil—between 4500 and 5000 miles. The procedure for changing the oil provided a step-by-step process to ensure the desired results—vehicle reliability and long life. How I do everything, from playing soccer to changing the oil, is generally what I classify as practices.

Instant Change—Change Without Practice

Most change cannot be bought. Instead, it must be taught. I have often been asked to supply an individual or company with the tools, guidelines, procedures, equipment, software, or hardware to create instant improvement. It frustrates me that people think they can purchase human change in the same way they can buy better equipment.

Scenario 1:

I will give you a million dollars if you can assure me that I'll wake up tomorrow with the ability to fluently read, write and speak Spanish.

Now that's not going to happen. It takes practice to learn a new way of doing something. Practice takes effort, passion and desire.

Scenario 2:

I bought the best golf clubs money can buy; I'll be a better golfer tomorrow.

That's not going to happen either, for the same reasons.

Scenario 3:

Let's bring in some experts to assist with this project. Asking employees who don't have experience working in a best-practice environment to write best-in-class guidelines and procedure isn't feasible.

Okay, this will work.

Programs

Programs are variations of guidelines and procedures that have been developed for everything from weight loss, to fitness training or learning a new language. Programs deliver expected results over a pre-determined time period, and are often used in the training or certification of people in certain tasks.

Effective Policy, Guideline and Procedure Writing

"For want of a nail, the shoe was lost;

For want of a shoe, the horse was lost;

For want of a horse, the rider was lost;

For want of a rider, the battle was lost;

For want of a battle, the kingdom was lost."

George Herbert

The development of guidelines and procedures follows the development of the workflow diagram.

Employees frequently turn to policy, guidelines and procedure documents to understand the internal processes of a department or company. Yet, those same employees are frequently frustrated because the document is so difficult to locate and comprehend. Good organization, clear language and accessible information are key elements to writing effective policies, guidelines and procedures. Keep the following points in mind:

- Determine the content required

- Organize the content so it's as clear and understandable as possible

- Always focus on the reader

- Write in plain English

- Be consistent and accurate

- Make the format as accessible as possible

In the quote above by George Herbert, we can see that the lack of a defined procedure can mean total loss of a desired goal. That's why you need a way to control and plan the development of policies, guidelines and procedures.

Document Control

Documents are the written policies, guidelines and procedures. How these documents are created and controlled for quality and integrity must be outlined in your administration plan. There is nothing more frustrating than to have inconsistency in document format, language or filing location.

Consider the following when you're developing your administrative plan:

- Format

- Layout

- Reference Numbers

- Electronic File Structure and Location

- Revision Numbers and Control

- Appendices

- Attachments

Guideline- and Procedure-Writing Software

There are a number of software packages on the market today for writing procedures and guidelines. Most have been developed to support ISO certification. I highly recommend using procedure- and guideline-writing software, both to ensure accuracy in development and to save valuable time in teaching everyone involved how to create styles, margins and document-related items associated with common word processing software applications such as Microsoft Word or IBM Lotus Notes.

Procedure-writing software works by providing standard electronic templates and forms. Anyone using it simply fills in the various text boxes associated with the electronic form to produce a report laid out in a standard format. Templates and forms can be modified to suit a specific business and managed electronically through a self-generated reference and cataloging number. If you are considering using procedure-writing software, make sure that it can generate Web documents. Many companies are making use of the Internet, intranets and LANs to store their policies, guidelines and procedures and make them accessible to their employees and shareholders.

Reference Manual

As the processes, policies, guidelines, procedures and programs are developed and designed, you should immediately file them in a manual for easy reference and for access during training. The project responsibilities matrix should identify who is responsible for developing and controlling the reference manual—preferably someone qualified and responsible.

Manual Format, Content and Control Considerations

Give some thought to the format, content and control of the reference manual. Manuals vary, in as many ways as there are business processes so there are a few rules to keep in mind:

- **FIRST**, if your company has already established a standard policy for manual format, content and control, it goes without saying that you should apply it.

- **SECOND**, many companies have registered with ISO (International Organization for Standardization), which has established standards for manuals and documents.

- **THIRD**, each manual must be designed to reflect the workflow elements and activities that support the business process.

- **FOURTH**, easy-to-read typefaces and font sizes, illustrations and diagrams should be large enough to see all the details.

- **FIFTH**, create and control the manual in a way that allows for easy updating.

Corporate Intranet and Hyperlinks

Many companies use an internal Web site (an intranet) to post training and reference manuals. Software used for Web page and document creation enables manuals to be available to everyone who has access to the

corporate intranet site. Use of hyperlinks and bookmarks allow users to quickly move to the relevant sections. Updates and revisions are simple to manage and control.

Table of Contents

When you set up the reference manual, include a table of contents that supports the business process workflow and functional areas.

Here is an example of a table of contents for warehouse materials management in a large production facility:

Chapter 6 Checklist: Design

1 Workflow and Process Mapping

☐ I have read and understand Workflow and Process Mapping.

☐ Yes, I have developed a workflow chart for our business process representing all functional area processes and integration.

Or ☐ No, a workflow chart is not applicable for my personal project.

2 Principles, Policies, Guidelines, Procedures, Practices and Programs

☐ I have read and understand Principals, Policies, Guidelines, Procedures, Practices and Programs.

3 Reference Manual

☐ I have read and understand the Reference Manual.

☐ Yes, I have created a reference manual.

☐ Yes, I have created the Table of Contents

☐ Yes, I have established the reference manual document control process

☐ Yes, I have established an electronic copy of the reference manual

☐ Yes, I have distributed the reference manual to the appropriate individuals or departments

Chapter 7
Orientation and Training

"You must be the change you wish to see in the world."

Mahatma Gandhi

The third phase of the Change Management Process Model™ begins with orientation and training. The objective here is to understand how to integrate the new materials, policies, guidelines, procedures and programs by everyone who will be affected.

As a change management consultant with a passion for instructing, it gives me great pleasure to write this chapter. Training is the force that keeps the words "successful" and "change" only one character space apart and prevents the combination from being an oxymoron.

Anytime you change the way something is done, you create a need for orientation, training and coaching—both for the employees affected, and for the change management team and supporting managers (see "The Change Management Team" in Chapter 4).

Let's look at the example of someone who takes the initiative to fulfill a dream of flying a plane. Clearly, orientation, training and coaching are a key part of turning that dream into reality. The orientation might consist of a facility tour, a walk around the aircraft and a thirty-minute introductory flight, during which the instructor points out the various instruments and safety features of the aircraft. Training consists of ground school, while coaching is done through a series of one-hour flights with a qualified instructor over a pre-determined period of time.

DIAGRAM: Stages of Orientation, Training and Coaching

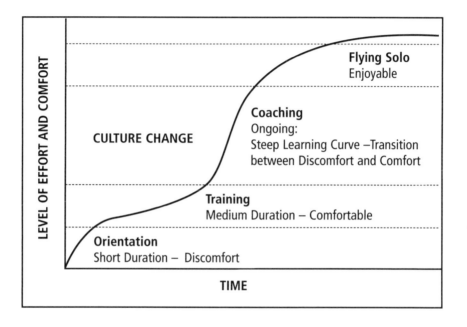

The above diagram illustrates the various stages of orientation, training and coaching with emphasis on the level of comfort. During orientation students tend to be overwhelmed by the new information. During training, however, they receive more materials that support what they learned during orientation, the explanations are more detailed, and there's time to absorb the information. This creates a more comfortable environment. Coaching may be a little uncomfortable at first when the students actually use the tools or practice a new procedure in a real-life setting. As they are coached and start to show improvement, they become more confident using their new skills or knowledge.

Orientation

Orientation prepares people for "what's coming down the line." During the planning and development phases, you used communication to keep everyone up to speed on the impending change, so they gained some idea of what to expect.

Orientation, however, provides a clearer picture by demonstrating the efforts of the planning and development phases. This is the time to share gap analysis results, workflow diagrams, guidelines and procedures, business process manuals and template tools.

Orientation Assembly

An orientation assembly conducted during working hours is an opportunity to gather everyone in one location and convey the progress and direction of your change improvement project. Make sure that the orientation is well prepared and executed. Time is critical: no more than two hours should be spent on orientation assemblies, including time at the end for questions and answers.

Orientation Symposium and Trade Show

An orientation symposium is an excellent opportunity to introduce everyone to a change improvement project, either during or after normal work hours. One preferred method is to reserve a large seminar room at a location off-site, such as a hotel, for two or three evenings and invite everyone to come on the evening that best suits their schedule. Have vendors involved in the project on hand to introduce new equipment, hardware or software and let staff try it out. Dinners, snacks, beverages and give-away items are popular at these events.

Training

A change improvement project fails to achieve the desired result most often because of a lack of training or coaching. Training is essential in the development phase of a change improvement project, and even more so during the implementation phase. It should include both the people leading the change as well as the people affected by it.

In many cases, the individuals involved in leading, managing and controlling the development phase are unfamiliar with the roles and responsibilities they have undertaken. Adjusting to a new order is even more difficult if you haven't been involved directly in the development phase, or worse, you knew nothing of the new order before it was implemented. Resistance to change is the direct result. Although it's not realistic to involve everyone in the development phase, it's also unrealistic to assume that everyone will adjust to change without sufficient training and orientation.

Who really benefits from training? In my years as an instructor of classroom workshops and seminars, I have come to believe there are four reasons why people request and attend training courses:

- To get away from their place of work and daily routine for a while. Especially if travel is involved, training courses are often viewed as a short vacation of sorts.

- To socialize with other people facing similar situations and work environment challenges.

- To add credentials to their resume.

- To learn more about a topic of interest so they can contribute more effectively or efficiently to the company they work for.

The better you understand these motivations, the better you can plan training, so let's look at them in more detail.

FIRST, getting away from the workplace routine can be an important part of training. In my experience, in-house training program participants aren't as enthusiastic and interested, primarily because they are too close to their workplace routine. They are often interrupted by phone calls or minor crises, and they know that they will have to put in additional hours after the training day is finished to deal with the most urgent tasks that have accumulated.

> *We all know a change is as good as a rest...*
>
> *as long as a rest is as good for a change.*

LIKEWISE, meeting people from other companies, environments or geographical areas is equally valuable. Bringing different people together to share their experiences can learn many things. The trick, however, is to ensure that when two or more individuals from one company attend a training workshop, they sit with people they don't know, instead of with their co-workers. Many benchmark initiatives have resulted from individuals meeting in this way.

THIRD, training does look good on a resume. It's a benefit employees appreciate.

FINALLY, it is quite reasonable to assume that participants are committed to change and will help develop and implement change opportunity initiatives for the benefit of their employer. Unfortunately, all too often they return to work following training only to find little recognition of their new training or qualifications. They hear remarks like, "okay, so you attended a training course, let's get on with our work" or "you're not going to change things around here just because you attended workshop."

Companies, leaders, supervisors and coaches must take advantage of the opportunity that training really provides. Recognize that employees have learned valuable things by giving them an option to develop or implement change. Individuals who attend training courses can pass on information; improve policies, guidelines and procedures; and coach other staff. Both the company and employee can benefit from training.

Types of Training

Training can take on a variety of formats. The primary objective is to make sure individuals understand a task or series of tasks so that they produce the outcome you're looking for. Training creates awareness and understanding and provides each individual with a certain level of comfort.

Classroom

Classroom-style training is by far the most popular method of training, either on its own or in combination with field training. If you choose this approach, keep the following tips in mind.

- **DO** restrict the size of the room size and the number of attendees. There is nothing more frustrating than to be crowded into a room that's too small or to feel uncomfortable about participating in a large group.

- **DO** attempt to enroll attendees who have similar backgrounds and experience in relation to the course content. A course aimed at too broad a range of people—such as ones provided by many training institutions—may not serve your best interests.

- **DO** stick to the agenda when you're instructing. Avoid the tendency to aim your teaching at the slowest participants. Other attendees will get bored and discouraged if too much time is spent trying to instruct a few individuals who seem to be struggling. Attendees will feel cheated if the full agenda of the course is not covered (especially if they paid to attend). Encourage anyone who is struggling to seek additional help after class.

- **DO** take a reasonable number of breaks. Many people are not used to sitting in one place hour after hour, so give them regular opportunities to get up and move around.

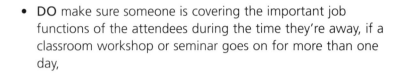

- **DO** make sure someone is covering the important job functions of the attendees during the time they're away, if a classroom workshop or seminar goes on for more than one day,

- **DON'T** let cell phones and pagers interrupt or distract the entire class. Ask everyone to turn them off at the beginning of each session.

Field

Field training is generally linked to classroom training and coaching. It may be short term or long term, depending on the topic. For example, short-term field training in fire fighting could involve a combination of in-class instruction and hands-on simulations where participants apply what they have learned in controlled conditions.

Long-term field training is where individuals or teams learn to apply their classroom training to real-life situations. The classroom training may last only a few days, while the field training could last anywhere from one month to two years.

Hands-on

Hands-on training has become extremely common in today's high-tech world, especially since the introduction of computers and technology hardware. For example, a trainer might coach an employee who is learning to use spreadsheets to create a departmental budget as he sits at the computer, doing the actual work.

Training Methodology and Development

Training program creation takes place during the development phase of your change improvement project. The training requirements should be based on the scope of your project and the assessment of who needs what training. You may decide to call on specialized organizations or consultants to help you with this task. If you have already hired a consulting firm to guide the change improvement project, chances are they can provide suitable training programs as well. (If not, you might want to ask yourself why.)

There are more and more training companies that recognize change management as an important area of opportunity, and it would be well worth investigating what they can offer. One starting point is *The Training Magazine* <www.trainingmag.com>, which specializes in training development.

Every job position demands specific knowledge and skills so our plan needs to identify those. It should specify what positions require training, what type of training and a schedule. Don't forget to include strategies for orientation and coaching.

The *orientation strategy* should include:

- The type of orientation required

- Who should conduct it (consultants, management, steering committee, etc.)

- The time, duration, location and agenda for each session

- Who should attend

- Method of announcement and follow-up

- A list of requirements to run the session, including support materials, equipment, transportation, accommodations, etc.

The *training strategy* should include:

- A description of the roles and responsibilities for each position and job function

- An assessment of the current knowledge and skills of all the individuals potentially affected by the change opportunity initiative

- The type of training required

- Who will conduct it, the number of instructors required, and what kind of qualification and experience the instructors should have

- The time, duration, location and agenda for each session

- Who should attend

- A training budget

The *coaching strategy* is discussed in detail in Chapter 9, "Control and Coaching."

Training Materials

The training plan includes identifying and developing training materials and establishing course content. Obviously, the extent of this effort will depend on the type of training required.

Materials are the vehicle for acquiring job knowledge and skills. They can be general overviews, site-specific procedures, simple checklists, or complex simulators. They can be paper-based, computer-based, group-oriented or self-study. Materials of various types can also be blended, so that, for example, a portion of the training is self-study and another portion is classroom-based.

Effective training materials need to appeal to a variety of learning styles, engage the audience, transmit information, reinforce learning and build job skills. Make sure they are geared to the reading level of your audience.

Paper-Based Materials

Traditional print-based materials are easily accessible and can include graphics and colour. Consider what format is most appropriate such as a three-ring binder, a glossy brochure, or a poster.

Computer-Based Materials

Multimedia or Internet-based training materials can include text, graphics, video and sound. Help files are useful for reference, as well as mastering the content and improving computer skills.

Existing Documentation

Existing reference manuals and site-specific drawings can be effective, low-cost alternatives to traditional materials, provided you have a good training plan and schedule.

Simulators

Practicing operations in a simulated environment provides hands-on experience without the costs or risk of real-life operations.

Games

Games can provide the most cost savings of all training tools available. I created a board game for a team of operations personnel that allowed them to become familiar with a new management process in a fun, non-threatening atmosphere. With each roll of the dice, they landed on one of the many activities identified in the process. Each player would then pick a

card that contained a short description of the activity and read it aloud to the rest of the group. Some cards provided opportunities to move to another activity, others created barriers or raised issues to consider.

Course Content

It should be clear from your training plan what content each course needs to deliver. Generally, it should be aimed at making sure employees can meet a specific target or achieve a certain required level of competency.

Certification Recognition and Qualification

Every year, thousands of employees attend training seminars and workshops to attain a new level of awareness and knowledge, and often they receive certificates of achievement upon completion. There is, however, a great deal of difference between being certified and being qualified.

Certification Recognition

Certification recognition—the presentation of a certificate to anyone who attends a scheduled training session—is a common practice. In some cases, any individual who registers and pays a fee can receive a certificate. (Honestly!) A certificate at the end of a workshop is a good way to recognize an individual's involvement, but it doesn't reflect how much was learned.

Certification Qualification

Certification qualification refers to the assessment of an individual's knowledge and skill based on the course content. It could include written, oral or practical tests, but the key idea is that candidates must achieve a certain level of competency in order to receive qualification.

While developing the training plan, you will need to consider whether certification recognition or qualification is more appropriate. I highly recommend that you establish some level of standard certification recognition and qualification for each training plan. In addition, all orientation, training and coaching should be divided into degrees of achievement.

Follow-up

Although follow-up is generally managed during the roll-out, control and coaching steps, it is critical to identify and address it at this stage.

Follow-up involves coaching individuals so that they become proficient in the new procedures you're implementing. Training programs alone are not enough in qualifying individuals.

When you develop your training plan, it is essential to identify how you will judge whether someone is qualified. This might include oral or written tests as well as hands-on exercises—the type of training will determine the kind of follow-up that is required. For example, if someone attends a training workshop on how to navigate a particular software application, the follow-up session might involve a hands-on exam. The most important thing to remember is that follow-up must be *continuous* and *recorded*. An individual's ability must be recognized, as well as their inability. The idea is to coach and follow up until the individual is confident and has the skills required to perform each function or activity at the highest level.

Follow-up can best be managed using a spreadsheet matrix identifying what guidelines, procedures or activities each individual is responsible for executing, and identifying the level of training and review. You can then establish a calendar for sessions and monitor it regularly so you know how each employee is progressing. From there, you can measure the performance of each employee as well as that of each team or department in delivering their product or service. You should measure the output of a business process against the input to accurately indicate performance.

Chapter 7 Checklist: Orientation and Training

1 Orientation

☐ I have read and understand Orientation.

2 Training

☐ I have read and understand Training.

3 Types of Training

☐ I have read and understood Types of Training.

4 Training Methodology and Development

☐ I have read and understand Training Development.

☐ Yes, I have developed a training plan.

Or ☐ No, a training plan is not applicable to my change project.

5 Certification Recognition and Qualification

☐ I have read and understand Certification Recognition and Qualification.

☐ Yes, I have included certification recognition and qualification in the training plan.

Or ☐ No, not certification and recognition are not applicable to my change project.

6 Follow-up

☐ I have read and understand Follow-up.

☐ Yes, I have included the follow-up information in my training plan.

Chapter 8
Roll-Out

"It is not necessary to change. Survival is not mandatory"

W. Edwards Deming

The second step in the implementation phase is roll-out. Once everyone affected by the change project has been oriented and trained, the new order of policies, guidelines, procedures, programs and materials can be put into practice.

"Training is a bridge named roll-out that spans the two worlds of change development and implementation"

E. J. Lister

Rolling Out Change

When we talk about *change to a way of doing something*, roll-out is the initial introduction out of a new service, or policy. *The roll-out of the new hotel policies is scheduled for next week.*

When we talk about *change to the way something looks or functions*, roll-out is the inaugural public exhibition of a new product. *The manufacturer's roll-out of the new jet is scheduled for next month.*

For the purpose of successful change management, roll-out refers to the introduction and establishment of new and improved policies, guidelines and procedures. It's the point where your change opportunity initiative will succeed or fail. This is when the majority of the plans you've developed are introduced, executed and, for the first time, function as part of the new order of business. Roll-out is a period of time when change is taking place in a controlled but flexible fashion, a period of testing and re-design, a period when the entire organization gets involved.

When an automobile manufacturer designs a new model vehicle, the general public isn't involved in the many months of design development. The same goes for the development phase of a change improvement project—it is just not practical to have everyone in the organization involved. That is why you establish a steering committee and change management team.

Once the development phase is competed, however, and you're ready for roll-out, you need a method of raising awareness. In the automobile example, the new model vehicle is promoted through media, shows and distribution. You may promote your change project differently; no matter how you do it, the new mode or new order of business must be made visible.

Roll-out can involve demonstration, communication, orientation, training and coaching. It provides a prototype, which you can then assess to see how easy or difficult it is to use, as well as how effective it is in meeting your performance targets.

Acceptance and Confidence

Acceptance is key—unless the individuals and business affected by the change accept it, your change project is jeopardized. Acceptance means understanding that the change will require effort, but will ultimately improve performance in one or more areas of life, work or business.

The Change Management Roll-out Maze

Let's compare the theory of workflow processes and guidelines to a maze. The maze has an entrance and an exit and between there are a number of paths you must choose between in order to successfully travel from the beginning to the end. Some paths lead to a dead end, while others return you to where you once were. Getting to the exit is a challenge for anyone with no previous experience or knowledge in traveling through the maze, especially if no maps are provided.

Coaching, which we discuss in the next chapter, will help everyone to negotiate the maze, but it's important to understand that the roll-out phase will likely involve some chaos and confusion.

Roll-out Timing and Duration

The timing and duration of the roll-out is critical. An attempt to roll-out too early may result in lack of sufficient documents, materials, training or equipment, while too late might result in lack of funding, lack of support or anticipation stress.

Often too much focus and funding effort is spent on the development phase, only to leave too little for the implementation phase.

How long the roll-out effort lasts obviously depends on the size and complexity of your change improvement project, but a few rules do apply. Make sure you develop the roll-out plan during the methodology step we discussed in Chapter 5. Second, divide the roll-out into smaller, more manageable and easily identified activities on the change improvement project schedule.

Roll-out Location

In many instances, more than one functional area or location will be expected to improve. For example, a large corporation with many manufacturing or production centers, franchise outlets, or offices may want to introduce and establish the new or improved policies, guidelines and procedures across the entire corporation. For reasons of management and control—and in most cases cost and resource restrictions as well— companies will choose to roll out changes at one location first. The chosen location will be more or less a prototype, where reaction and results will be closely monitored and measured.

To ensure the highest rate of success, it is critical that staff at this first location is aware of the change improvement project and have a supportive attitude. A location that has managed change successfully in the past is even better. Other factors to consider are geographic location, facility size and the number of employees. As part of the roll-out plan, you'll need to identify which sites will be included and which one to be scheduled first. As individuals become involved and familiar with the process, you can use their experience and enthusiasm to assist with the roll-out of future sites.

If you've successfully communicated how the change improvement project can improve existing situations, it's not unusual for several sites to request implementation and roll-out. Managers at all levels, in all locations, will be eager to initiate positive change. Remember that the success of implementation depends on the expertise of the individuals involved in the development phase. Be cautious not to overextend your team members' abilities with this new order of business.

Chapter 8 Checklist: Roll-out

1 Rolling Out Change

☐ I have read and understand Rolling Out Change.

2 Roll-out Timing and Duration

☐ I have read and understand Roll-out Timing and Duration.

☐ Yes, I have established the timing and duration of the roll-out step.

3 Roll-out Location

☐ I have read and understand Roll-out Location.

☐ Yes, I have chosen a roll-out location.

☐ Yes, I have conducted orientation as per the training plan.

☐ Yes, I have conducted the training program as per the training plan.

☐ Yes, I have certified and recognized individual and group achievements.

Chapter 9
Control and Coaching

"If you don't like something, change it. If you can't change it, change your attitude. Don't complain."

Maya Angelou

The fourth phase of the Change Management Process Model™ is management. The first step of the management phase is control and coaching. The objective here is to understand how to coach individuals to support the learning and guide the transition from current practices to best practices, while controlling the outcome.

Performance Management

Performance management is a large and complicated topic. You can find thousands of tools, consultants and books dedicated to this topic alone. However, in this chapter we'll explore performance management only as it applies to change management and project management, where it's important to measure the status of project key performance targets, indicators and change outcomes.

Successful change is not simply about controlling resources and intangible assets during the life cycle of the project itself, but also ensuring that the on-going practices of the new order fulfill the project's mission.

When it comes to managing human resources, performance management involves comparing input effort to the output results of an activity or procedure.

Business profitability depends on the performance of five primary types of assets: raw materials or inventory, equipment assets, human resources, financial resources, and market customers. In order to deliver a quality product or service and maintain or gain market share, these primary resources must perform at a level of excellence. It is the responsibility of business leaders and managers to use them as wisely as possible by measuring the level of performance of each one and minimizing waste and loss.

Performance is a result of design and practice. The activities and procedures we practice, and the guidelines and policies under which we practice them, must be designed to produce excellent and consistent results.

Measuring Performance

Any change that's intended to enhance performance, whether it's the performance of employees or other assets, must be measurable so that you can determine how effective the change was and identify possibilities for continuous improvement. Measuring the performance of production assets is commonplace—perhaps because the impact of an assembly line breakdown is so clear—and seems to take precedence over measuring human resource performance. Of course it is easier to measure how well equipment performs compared to employees, but the difficulty doesn't make it any less important.

DIAGRAM: Measuring the Performance of a Task

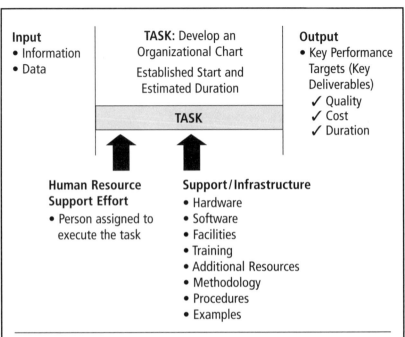

Input
• Information
• Data

TASK: Develop an Organizational Chart

Established Start and Estimated Duration

TASK

Output
• Key Performance Targets (Key Deliverables)
  ✓ Quality
  ✓ Cost
  ✓ Duration

Human Resource Support Effort
• Person assigned to execute the task

Support/Infrastructure
• Hardware
• Software
• Facilities
• Training
• Additional Resources
• Methodology
• Procedures
• Examples

Performance is measured with the expectation that 100% output results will be achieved. However, in the absence of trained, qualified staff, or sufficient support/infrastructure, it will be impossible to achieve a 100% output. Measuring the performance however can easily be accomplished and the problem area(s) can be identified, i.e. lack of input information of data, lack of qualified human resources, lack of software, hardware, training, procedures, etc.

When you're implementing a change improvement project, you need to know that everyone is recognizing and accepting change and learning any new or modified tasks that are involved. You also need to know how that change is affecting your output results. Even after the change has been implemented, it may still need more modification. This is continuous improvement working at its best.

When you're measuring asset performance, keep in mind:

Production Assets

- Availability

- Reliability

Human Resources

- Direct–Production Staff

- Indirect–Overhead Management

Performance Reviews Versus Performance Measurement

Annual *performance reviews* are a common way to analyze performance by determining how well an employee fulfilled the roles and responsibilities of his or her position and evaluating personal commitment, attendance, attitude and contribution to the organization.

I mention performance reviews here for the sole purpose of asking you not to use this method to measure business output. Performance reviews should be used solely for assessing achievements with regard to personal, work and career related goals and objectives, either in support of the company or the individuals themselves. They are not an effective way to measure how well an employee performs the daily, weekly and monthly activities identified in the relevant business processes; performance checklists are better for this.

Measuring performance means gathering factual information: what I put in, what I got out, what inefficiencies are occurring, what is working, what is broken.

The cause of poor performance often lies with the management process rather than with the individual. As we discussed in "Recognizing Change Improvement Opportunities" in Chapter 3, if you're not getting the result you want, you need to ask: "*What broke?*" Did the individual not understand the task, is the procedure associated with the task not sufficient, or is there a bottleneck in the business process?

The bottom line is that there is no guesswork. If I have an employee who is spending 12 hours a day at the office to complete the tasks associated for an 8-hour-a-day position, something is wrong. Chances are the tasks are not very well defined, or they are well defined but not understood, or simply, there are too many tasks assigned to be completed in the allotted time. If the tasks are well defined, the individual understands them and has the skills and knowledge to perform them, and the tasks are not too many to be executed and completed in the allotted time, then the issue could be poor personal management, poor attitude, a problem in the business process, or lack of support from managers who are not performing *their* tasks in accordance with the business process.

Performance Checklists

Creating performance checklists, observing and providing feedback, and conducting appraisals enable you to achieve the best results by measuring how well employees are performing the tasks they've been assigned.

Performance checklists detail tasks to be performed in a specified time period, along with specific quality results. These should relate directly to an employee's roles and responsibilities, such as authorizing expenditures, analyzing data, engineering, selling, shipping, etc., and indirectly related tasks such as meetings, training, paperwork, phone calls, etc.

To begin the process, you and the employee should work together to develop the performance checklists. The lists help the employee to focus on achieving specific results to support the desired output of a given business process. Discuss goals and objectives throughout the year, providing a framework to ensure that employees achieve results through coaching and mutual feedback.

Let's look at the example of preparing an aircraft for departure. To avoid any flight delays, the individuals responsible for loading, stocking, cleaning and fueling the aircraft must execute their tasks efficiently. At the same time, they must be careful not to forget anything—a team that loads meals onto the plane very quickly is efficient, but if they forget a meal item, they won't be very effective. If they follow a checklist, it can be reviewed after the plane leaves to measure performance: whether each task has been completed in the estimated time (efficiency), and whether anything was overlooked (effectiveness).

DIAGRAM: Sample Performance Checklist

	Task ✚	Estimate	Actual	Responsibility	Status
1	⊟ **FLIGHT LOGISTICS CHECKLIST**	**90**	**80**		**Check**
2	⊟ **Cleaning Crew**	**30**	**30**	**Clean Air**	**Check**
3	Empty garbage and recycle bins	10	10		Check
4	Vacuum and clean washrooms	20	20		Check
5	Replace flight information cards and magazines	20	20		Check
6	⊟ **Baggage Handlers**	**90**	**80**	**Smith**	**Check**
7	Load cargo and baggage	90	90		Check
8	⊟ **Fueling**	**40**	**40**	**Jones**	**Check**
9	Load fuel	40	40		Check
10	⊟ **Meals**	**30**	**30**	**Jules**	**Check**
11	Deliver/load meals	30	30		Check
12	⊟ **Logistics**	**60**	**60**	**Reed**	**Check**
13	Empty waste management system	10	10		Check
14	Load consumables	60	60		Check

Key Performance Indicators

To know if you are moving in the direction of positive change (staying on the course you've mapped out), you need to know the status of your project, so you can compare where you are currently to where you should be.

To manage change successfully, you must be able to measure it. Performance can be measured by a number of indicators, so you must decide which key indicators you wish to use. Keep in mind that these will differ from project to project.

Typical key indicators involve time (project duration) and cost. It's also essential to include an indication of how well you are meeting your stated vision (goals and objectives), and how well you are staying on track with your promise to deliver a good or service (mission).

Once you've determined the key indicators, targets can be established. For example, in my personal life I have a plan to improve my health by losing weight. My goal is to lose 30 pounds in the next six months. My objective is to lose 1–1.5 pounds per week. My key project indicator will be to measure my weight, and my target will be my desired weight (which I'm not willing to divulge!).

Once a project is complete, you'll need a new set of indicators and targets to ensure your mission continues to be fulfilled—at this point, measuring project cost and duration is no longer relevant. For example, if the mission of a hotel were to greet each customer in a friendly and efficient manner, the key indicator would measure customer feedback. Other indicators could be room preparation quality and time, and room occupancy rates. Once you've established key indicators and determined realistic targets, you've set yourself up for employee recognition, self-confidence and continuous improvement.

Coaching

Coaching is the act of providing support to individuals or groups to decrease their learning curve and help them produce the best results possible. The term is best recognized from competition, where individuals and teams are trained, oriented, prepared and drilled to produce consistent "best in class" results, but it's equally applicable to business.

Coaching is a method of strengthening communication between you and the employee. It helps to shape performance and increase the likelihood that the employee's results will meet your expectations. It also increases employee motivation, commitment and self-esteem. Coaching sessions provide you and the employee with an opportunity to discuss his or her progress toward meeting mutually established standards and goals.

A consultant or team leader can coach members of the change management team with their individual tasks during the planning and development phases. Coaching is especially important during the implementation phase as part of the training and roll-out strategy. It follows orientation and training, where the learning curve becomes increasingly steep, requiring on-going instruction and positive feedback.

Been There, Done That!

Who wants to be coached by someone who hasn't experienced the steep learning curve or fear and discomfort that change brings? Let's face it: training can be done by anyone who feels confident enough to read and understand something and pass it on, without necessarily having any practical experience. The same is not true with coaching. Coaching is three things: passing on learned experiences, expressing a positive attitude, and providing honest feedback and encouragement.

Successful change is dependent on *letting go of the old* and trusting in the new order of business, and a good coach can make sure that happens.

Coaching Strategy

Your coaching strategy should be determined during the development of the orientation and training plan. It should include:

- Coaching requirements by functional area or by guidelines and procedures. It is rare that one person is qualified or experienced enough in the guidelines and procedures for every functional area to provide effective support. Therefore, each functional area must be identified, combined where appropriate, and aligned with a qualified coach. For example, safety may need a specialized coach, whereas someone else may handle both maintenance and inventory.

- A matrix of individuals who require coaching. This matrix should indicate the areas in which they require coaching and the level of qualification they are expected to achieve.

- A schedule indicating the length of the program or number of sessions.

- Duration of each coaching session.

- Location of coaching.

- Coaching materials and equipment requirements. Many situations require specialized materials and equipment, such as computers, simulators, and tools.

- An assessment schedule identifying when the individuals or groups being coached should be evaluated, and what level of performance they should be expected to achieve. This could involve oral, written or practical testing.

Observation and Feedback

Once you have established objectives and standards, you should observe employees' performance and provide feedback. You have a responsibility to recognize and reinforce strong performances, and to identify and encourage improvement where it is needed.

Provide informal feedback almost every day. By observing and giving thoughtful detailed feedback, you play a critical role in each employee's continued success and motivation to meet performance expectations.

Key Elements of Coaching

To make your session effective, you must understand the key elements of coaching:

- Observe the employee's work and solicit feedback from others.

- When the employee's performance is successful, take the time to understand why.

- Advise the employee ahead of time that you'd like to discuss a specific issue.

- Focus attention on only one or two specific aspects of the employee's performance in a single session, unlike a performance review.

- Recognize successes and improvements. Use reinforcement techniques to shape behavior.

- Focus on behavior, not personality.

- Ask the employee for help in identifying and resolving problems. Use active listening to show you understand.

- Discuss alternative solutions.

- Agree on the action to be taken. Set specific goals and maintain communication.

- Schedule follow-up meetings to measure results.

- Document key elements of the coaching session.

Questions to Consider When Coaching

To provide effective feedback, you must understand the elements of performance and analyze when it is marginal. Keep these questions in mind:

- How is the employee expected to perform?

- Does the employee understand these expectations? If not, why not?

- Does the employee know what successful results look like? How do you know?

- Does the employee know his or her performance is marginal? How do you know?

- Are there obstacles beyond the employee's control? Can you remove them?

- Has the employee ever performed this task satisfactorily?

- Is the employee willing and able to learn?

- Does satisfactory performance result in excessive work being assigned?

- Does unsatisfactory performance result in positive consequences such as an undesirable task being reassigned?

During the Coaching Session

If you conduct a coaching session to *provide positive feedback* to the employee, keep the following ideas in mind:

- Describe the positive result or work habit using specific details.

- Solicit your employee's opinion of the result or work habit.

- Ask the employee to identify elements that contributed to success (such as adequate time or resources, support from management or other employees, the employee's talent and interest in the project).

- Discuss ways in which you and the employee can support continued positive results.

- Reinforce the value of the work and describe how it fits in with the goals of the work unit or department.

- Show your appreciation of the positive results and your confidence that the employee will continue to perform satisfactorily.

- If appropriate, document your discussion for the employee's file.

When you conduct a coaching session to *improve performance*, you may want to use the following format:

- Describe the issue or problem, referring to specific behaviors.

- Involve the employee in the problem-solving process.

- Discuss the causes of the problem.

- Identify and write down possible solutions.

- Decide on specific actions to be taken by each of you.

- Agree on a follow-up date.

- Document key elements of the session.

If your coaching session is conducted to *address poor work habits* such as continued tardiness, keep these steps in mind:

- Describe in detail the poor work habit that was observed.

- Say why it concerns you.

- Ask why it occurred and listen non-judgmentally to the explanation. Describe the need for change and ask for ideas.

- Discuss each idea and offer your help.

- Agree on specific actions to be taken and set a specific follow-up date.

- Document results from the session.

Follow-up Discussion

To conduct a follow-up discussion, consider the following steps:

- Review the previous discussion(s).

- If the employee's performance hasn't improved sufficiently, discuss this and ask for reasons why.

- Indicate what the consequences will be if the employee's performance doesn't improve. (No threats! This isn't an oral warning.)

- Agree on action to be taken and set a follow-up date, if appropriate.

- Convey your confidence in the employee.

- Document your discussion.

Project Status and Updates

The management phase of the change improvement project focuses primarily on controlling and coaching. Unlike the planning, development and implementation phases that have defined beginnings and endings, one following after the other with little or no overlap, the management phase spans almost the entire length of the Change Management Process. This is because you need to manage and control the entire project from identification through to continuous improvement. That means updating the various activities identified in the change improvement project on a regular basis so you can identify any variance between the goals and objectives and the earned value of the project itself.

Managing Changes to the Project's Scope of Work

In change management seminars, I asked senior managers and business owners to discuss with their team members what they would do better on their next change improvement project. *"Manage project scope of work changes"* was third on the list.

I'm not aware of a single project where the original scope of work did not change at one time or another either by expanding the work involved or increasing the cost, or both. *Before* this happens, you need to establish a method of managing these changes.

Changing the scope of work is different from failing to meet a project schedule, which is the result of poor performance, planning or estimating. Changes to the scope of work typically involve adjustments in the definition or duration of an activity to accommodate additional work. This could be due to:

- Additional training requirements

- Additional hardware, software and equipment needs

- Recognition of additional work events or actions

The planning phase is the time to establish a process for managing changes to the scope of work. This could be an individual or team assignment and should be identified in the project responsibilities matrix.

Performance and Project Variance

Performance does not affect the scope of work associated with a project either positively or negatively; however, it does affect its progress.

Performance is a measure of what has actually been expended, in terms of work hours or operating costs, measured against what has been earned, based on your estimates of tasks or activity completion.

For example, if you estimated a task would take 400 hours of work effort to produce the desired results, but it actually took 500 hours; measuring performance will uncover the variance. Simply put, it took 100 additional work effort hours, times the cost, to produce the results that you estimated would take 400 work effort hours. This could be attributed to poor planning, estimating, or execution. If you perform a forecast and trend analysis early in the project, you can project the overruns and identify opportunities to take corrective action. However, if you are not monitoring the status of completed work and actual time and cost, you could be heading for a surprise at the end of the tunnel.

Performance plays a key role in both the Change Management Process and the day-to-day management of personal, work and business activities. From the beginning of the change opportunity initiative, you need to measure how well the transformation is progressing and how well practices are changed as a result. Since poor performance in any area is often the main reason to change, performance itself can stand alone as a method for identifying new opportunities.

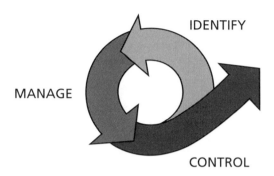

Together, change management, performance management and project management create the circle of identify, manage and control that will ensure a successful outcome, as shown in the RAC (Recognition and Acceptance of Change) picture.

Productivity Versus Performance

Productivity and performance have two very different meanings. *Productivity* is a factor that you apply to a baseline or benchmark estimate when you're developing a project plan. It reflects how much experience or knowledge someone has—or doesn't have—that will determine how effectively he or she can perform the specified task. *Performance* measures how well the task was executed compared to the estimated baseline or benchmark.

Let's look at the example of a change improvement project that calls on employees to learn a new software package. You would need to apply a productivity factor to your baseline or benchmark standards to make sure you're evaluating employee progress and performance success fairly, since obviously it will take time before they can use the new software effectively. The steeper the learning curve, the larger the productivity factor should be.

Chapter 9 Checklist: Control and Coaching

1 Performance Management

☐ I have read and understand Performance Management.

2 Key Performance Indicators

☐ I have read and understand Key Performance Indicators.

☐ Yes, I have established key performance indicators.

☐ Yes, I have been monitoring and controlling the project with key performance indicators and weekly project status and updates.

3 Coaching

☐ I have read and understand Coaching.

☐ Yes, I have been coaching on a regular basis as per the coaching plan.

4 Project Status and Updates

☐ I have read and understand Project Status and Updates.

☐ Yes, I have been tracking project status and updates on a weekly basis.

5 Managing Changes to the Project's Scope of Work

☐ I have read and understand Managing Changes to the Project's Scope of Work.

☐ Yes, I have established a process for managing changes to the scope of work.

6 Performance and Project Variance

☐ I have read and understand Performance and Project Variance.

Chapter 10
Continuous Improvement

"All men dream, but unequally. Those that dream at night in the dusty recesses of their minds awake the next day to find that their dreams were just vanity. But those who dream during the day with their eyes wide open are dangerous men; they act out their dreams to make them reality."

Thomas Edward Lawrence (Lawrence of Arabia)

The final step in the Change Management Process Model™ is continuous improvement. The object here is to understand how to establish a program to dynamically assess the results of your change initiative so that you can build on its success and ensure ongoing improvement.

The Continuous Improvement Process

Continuous improvement is as essential for individual and business survival and growth as is change. One does not exist without the other. Continuous improvement will support the development and implementation phases of your change project and give you a method of continually modifying and updating activities associated with the resulting business process.

A continuous improvement process provides a method of identifying and requesting change modifications, and then analyzing, developing, implementing, monitoring and controlling these change modifications. In a sense, it's comparable to the change management process itself, except that it focuses primarily on proactive change.

Employees are often quick to disparage any new practice that they haven't been involved in developing. Establishing a process that encourages and empowers shop floor staff to make things work better offers three advantages. First, it reduces the resistance to change; second, it improves the practice; and third, it gives employees credit for creating improvement, which boosts overall motivation and morale.

Many times I have heard employees say, "That'll never work" before they even try a new process. Then they try it and say, "See, I told you it wouldn't work, you should have done it this way". So I reply, "Great, let's try it your way," and they usually jump on board.

You'll need to establish a clear method for employees to communicate their ideas for improvement. A suggestion box or a form that can be filled in and sent to the continuous improvement team could be used. Without a way to express their ideas, employees will continue to criticize rather than assist with improvement.

Organizations dedicated to continuous improvement create and maintain programs that support changes to current practices and that help individuals fulfil the organization's mission. They create and maintain systems that allow and encourage all employees to work together, to use data and problem-solving tools to improve the way they do things, and to find ways to do things better every day. Individuals dedicated to continuous improvement regularly monitor their actions and reactions and measure them against their stated mission.

Remember, the continuous improvement process is a vehicle for the enhancements that flow from your project. A manufacturing company I was working with implemented a series of new practices for improving production line efficiencies, with immediate results. However, a specific practice produced only a slight increase in performance. An employee pointed out that a slight modification to a procedure would have a positive effect and once the procedure was rewritten and implemented, performance shot up to the desired level. Thanks to the continuous improvement process that was established during the management phase of the project, a number of changes were made to the process and related procedures over the next few months that led to performance results that were even better than expected.

Learned Experiences and the Change Management Process

"Words of inspiration are conceived at the moment of learned experience."

E.J. Lister

You may not find happiness living in the past, but by learning from it you may find happiness in the future. Learned experiences offer valuable opportunities for improvement. The phrase "Those who ignore history are doomed to repeat it" is valid. That's why we should review what history has taught us and apply it to our environments to create proactive change.

At one point or another, most individuals and businesses have been through changes that didn't produce the expected or desired results. In this situation you don't need to assess current practices; the below-average results themselves signal an opportunity for improvement.

To take advantage of learned opportunities, it is important to document the activity or series of activities that produced less-than-desirable results. The act of improvement may be as simple as modifying a procedure or creating a new one, or as complicated as establishing a change improvement project.

Following the Change Management Process

You are not going to get everything right the first time—even the best planned and executed change improvement projects require modifications and updates. Typically, you'll identify the need for these once you've begun to put a procedure into action. This is normal, and it's why continuous improvement is part of the Change Management Process.

Learning from Others

Learning from experience is not limited to your own. Base your successes on others, and learn from those who share similar interests.

For example, the strategies I use to conduct my training workshops came primarily from an individual whom I was fortunate enough to work with. He had developed the procedures over a number of years and generously shared them with me, bringing me success much sooner and with much less effort than if I had been obliged to create my own from scratch.

You can also see plenty of examples in the business world. For instance, once Chrysler pioneered the minivan and proved there was a market for it, other companies built on that success with much less effort and risk.

Cause-and-Effect Diagrams

Cause-and-effect diagrams—also known as fish bone diagrams because their box and line structure resemble the head and spine of the fish—help you to think through causes of a problem thoroughly. Considering all possible causes of the problem, rather than just the ones that are most obvious, is a major benefit.

Here's how it works:

1. Identify the problem.

Write down the problem you face in a box on the left-hand side of a large sheet of paper. Where appropriate, identify who is involved, what the problem is, and when and where it occurs. Then draw a line across the paper horizontally from the box. This gives you space to develop ideas.

2. Work out the major factors involved.

Next identify the factors that may contribute to the problem. Draw a line off the spine for each factor and label it. These may be people involved with the problem, systems, equipment, materials, external forces, etc. Using the "fish bone" analogy, the factors you identify are the bones of the fish. Think of as many as possible. If you are trying to solve the problem as a team, this may be a good time for some brainstorming.

3. Identify possible causes.

For each factor you listed, brainstorm the possible causes of the problem that may be related to it. For example, if you identified people as a major factor, consider why they are contributing to the problem. Was there a lack of training? Poorly defined goals? High turnover? Show these as smaller lines coming off the "bones" of the fish. If a cause is large or complex, break it down into sub-causes. Show these as lines coming off each cause line.

4. Analyze your diagram.

> Once you have a diagram showing all the possible causes of
> your problem, investigate and carry out assessments to learn a
> little more about the most likely causes, and then begin
> developing solutions.

The example below shows a cause-and-effect diagram drawn by a
businesswoman who is experiencing trouble getting customers to walk in
the door:

DIAGRAM: Sample Cause-and-Effect

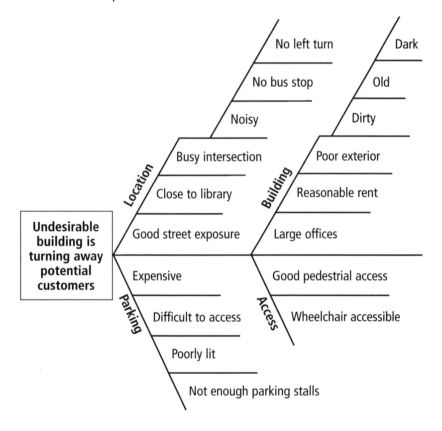

If this woman had not thought the problem through, she might have assumed that the building in which her business was established was the real cause. Instead, the diagram makes it clear that parking and a tricky intersection are the real issues. Her next step might be to arrange a meeting with city staff to discuss increasing the parking and improving the intersection.

You can use a cause-and-effect diagram to:

- Sort and segregate the possible causes of a problem into a logical order

- Identify what data needs to be gathered

- Educate participants in the problem-solving process

- Guide discussions and keep meetings on target

- Create a complete project management tool that displays actions taken and results achieved

Implementing Continuous Improvement

While introducing continuous improvement to reduce waste and increase performance is a great idea, I believe most businesses introduce it too early. If you have few defined business processes, procedures or guidelines, it is difficult to identify *what* to improve. Without defined processes, policies and procedures, every individual will practice and perceive their activities and responsibilities differently. And every individual will think his or her way is okay. "Improve what?" they all say.

For continuous improvement to be successful, it needs to be accepted as an on-going part of everyday life and the business environment. In a business environment, this typically means creating a continuous improvement team that provides a focal point for change suggestions and initiatives. Being part of the team does not have to be a full-time commitment, nor does it have to be long-term. The continuous improvement team can very well be a continuation of the change management team, with a new agenda and schedule.

Essentially, the team is responsible for reviewing suggestions, recommending improvements, and assigning responsibility to individuals, teams or departments to ensure the continuous improvement process is followed correctly.

Chapter 10 Checklist: Continuous Improvement

1 The Continuous Improvement Process

☐ I have read and understand The Continuous Improvement Process.

2 Learned Experiences and the Change Management Process

☐ I have read and understand Learned Experiences and the Change Management Process.

3 Implementing Continuous Improvement

☐ I have read and understand Implementing Continuous Improvement.

☐ Yes, I have established a continuous improvement process.

☐ Yes, I have established a continuous improvement team.

☐ Yes, I understand the need to continually seek opportunities for improvement.

Part III   CONCLUSION

Chapter 11
The Organizational Impact of Performance Change

"If you want to make enemies, try to change something."

Woodrow Wilson

Although humans are complicated, inconsistent and sometimes irrational, they are one of a business's most valuable assets. They are also the asset that is emotionally affected by change and, all too often, the asset that is replaced or let go in an effort to increase bottom-line performance.

This isn't a book about organizational restructuring or downsizing, but I've included this chapter because a change in corporate policies, guidelines or procedures may require a change to the corporate organization at one level or another. This in turn may mean redesigning organizational structures and adjusting the number of employees to support the new order.

The intention of this chapter is not to focus directly on organizational change, but rather to view it as a possibility you need to keep in mind.

Sizing—The Right Fit

Whether you call it downsizing or right-sizing, the goal is the same: to match the number of employees in the organization to the tasks and responsibilities required to do business effectively and efficiently.

To decide how many employees your organization needs, you'll have to quantify the business from top to bottom. This is quite simple in a small business. However, as a business matures, it becomes looser. Neglect and waste become evident as parts of the business gradually begin to perform less efficiently. Controlling, managing, and even understanding every aspect of the business becomes an impossible task.

When an established company makes the shift from current practices to best practices, unfortunately it often involves staff reduction. On the other hand, a new company or business that establishes best-practice policies and procedures from the beginning can hire the right number of staff, contracting additional resources only when the output goals demand it.

Job Descriptions

To specify the scope of human resource effort required to perform a specific job, you'll need to create a written description. This job description should identify each task the employee must accomplish. For example, an automobile mechanic's position would involve several dozen tasks, from diagnosing problems correctly following a specified procedure to filling out the "work performed" portion of the work order after completing each repair.

The list of tasks that make up the job description must support the business process, which means you need to review, create or modify them during or immediately following any change improvement project. As we discussed earlier, tasks are procedures practiced within established guidelines. If the job task is not aligned with the procedures you've established, or worse yet, the job description doesn't contain the procedure-related task, you can't expect that procedure to be practiced, at least not consistently.

If the change project results in a new job, you'll need to create a job description from scratch and then go through the usual process of finding someone to fill it.

Job Assessments

With guidelines and procedures in place and linked to a specific job, you'll need to regularly assess how well an individual executes each task. You no longer need to judge someone's performance based on his or her ability to outperform another. That's because you know that if the individual is qualified to perform the tasks related to the job description, and if the tasks were developed from best practices, the results will be as good as expected. Regardless of your employees' attitudes or dispositions, when they practice the procedures within the specified guidelines, everyone will be rewarded with best-practice achievement.

I have heard many times that you should never purchase a vehicle that was assembled on a Monday, because an individual's attitude and temperament is generally poorer following the weekend and the result can be a problem-prone car. However, if the manufacturer has established best-practice guidelines and procedures and the employees have been trained in defined job-related tasks, there won't be any poor-quality vehicles produced—the system simply will not allow for below-average results.

Investing in Training

Employees are a company's most valuable assets and should be compensated accordingly. Compensation refers to the wages and benefits, such as a pension plan or dental coverage that a company trades for the services of an individual. Essentially, the company is investing in an individual by providing a paycheck and a benefits package. In return, a company should expect to benefit financially, economically and physically.

One of the greatest investments for a company is in training an employee. Training benefits both the employer and the employee. Training allows the employee to contribute better to the company's bottom line, to advance and receive even more compensation based on his or her increased value to the company.

The training programs outlined in Chapter 7, *"Orientation and Training"* can be established in a more accurate and precise manner once the job description has been created. For obvious reasons it is easier and more effective to train someone in a task that's clearly defined.

Passion and Performance

Anyone can be and should be passionate about something, and individuals should be recognized for his or her passion. It's passion that makes heroes, wonderful friends, partners and lovers and above all, individuals capable of producing above-average results. Imagine how a company would prosper if all employees had jobs that matched their desire.

Having passion, or being passionate, is a characteristic that must be identified within every individual. I read somewhere that every human being should have something to do, something to love and something to look forward to. When people discuss with me their total lack of interest in their present situation, be it work, relationship, health, finance or business, my first response is to ask them what they are passionate about.

My wife Toonie is passionate about her horses. Since the age of thirteen she has cared for and ridden one horse or another. Through all of her teenage years and her working life and now into retirement, she has owned and cared for a horse. During her 21-year career as an RCMP constable, she worked shift work and relocated five times, but never once lost her passion for horses. Even today she seldom misses a day of grooming or riding. I admire her for her passion; I still find it truly attractive and inspirational.

When you're establishing, re-structuring or re-organizing a business, try to take passion into account. Whenever possible, match an individual's beliefs and passions to the appropriate tasks.

Roles and Responsibilities

Physical assets provide job consistency as long as a constant energy source is provided and the equipment is operated and maintained within the design parameters. The same is not true when we deal with people. Yet if an employee doesn't perform a task consistently, it will hurt business output.

That's why you need to establish a method of ensuring certain performance levels for each position, based on the job description, roles, responsibilities and established practices. You can measure key performance targets associated with the established practices, tasks and activities using key performance indicators on a weekly or daily basis. Checklists are a helpful tool for doing this.

Chapter 11 Checklist:
The Organizational Impact of Performance Change

1 Sizing–The Right Fit

☑ I have read and understand Sizing—The Right Fit.

☑ Yes, I am currently working with Human Resources to resize our organization to best fit the established business processes.

2 Job Descriptions

☑ I have read and understand Job Descriptions.

3 Job Assessments

☑ I have read and understand Job Assessments.

4 Investing in Training

☑ I have read and understand Investing in Training.

5 Passion and Performance

☑ I have read and understand Passion and Performance.

6 Roles and Responsibilities

☑ I have read and understand Roles and Responsibilities.

Part IV   CASE STUDIES

Chapter 12
Manufacturing–A Case Study

*"If we don't change, we don't grow.
If we don't grow, we aren't really living."*

Gail Sheehy

The following case study demonstrates the success achieved by a manufacturing company using the Change Management Process Model.™ Each step of the model is briefly explained as it occurred in a real-life environment. You may wish to return to previous chapters, as you read through this case study to better understand how each phase and supporting step was used.

Background

A soft drink manufacturing company, Tiger Cola (a pseudonym), had a long-established brand name in the soft drink industry and a large market share. Although demand for its product was high and it received large orders for each product in its line, senior managers at Tiger Cola recognized that they were compromising on profits. Problems with raw material deliveries, mechanical breakdowns and poor distribution procedures were costing them money. In 2001, they hired me as a consultant to help manage a change project that would address these problems.

Corporate Strategy (Strategic Plan)

The company had established a strategic plan earlier in the year that supported its existing corporate vision and mission statement. A great deal of effort was placed on assessing and analyzing potential external situations that might place Tiger Cola in a reactive change environment. Senior management considered current trends in the soft drink industry, possible new trends and products, consumer lifestyles, economic predictions, future population projections, potential new distributors and retailers, the cost and procurement of raw materials, taxes, labor, capital asset replacement and many other issues that might provide opportunities for proactive change.

The corporation had done everything right to prevent unexpected external change, but what it hadn't done was incorporate methods of avoiding unexpected internal change. It had not predicted problems with the reliability of its capital assets or inefficient employee performance.

It was clear that the corporation had to establish better internal practices if it was to remain competitive and profitable and maintain shareholder confidence. This meant taking a good look at both the core business process and the supporting processes within the corporation.

Planning Phase

Identification

Business Process Assessments and
Gap Analysis / Benchmarking

To determine which department or functional area would benefit the most from changes—that is, create the greatest improvement in product quality and quantity with the least amount of resource effort—I was hired as an independent change management consultant. My task was to review Tiger Cola's current practices in each department and functional area using a business process assessment survey. I measured current practices against benchmarked best practices within the soft drink manufacturing industry, and assessed the following departments and functional areas:

- Warehousing
- Maintenance
- Operations
- Sales and Marketing
- Distribution
- Safety
- Quality Control
- Accounting
- Research and Development

The results of the assessment survey showed that maintenance, operations and quality control did not have sufficient guidelines and procedures in place to allow them to achieve a best-in-class status. Furthermore, the existing guidelines and procedures were not being used consistently. Production line efficiencies were low, with an average throughput of only 63%. Equipment reliability and worker performance were difficult to measure due to insufficient data. However, it was clear that the lack of guidelines and procedures for maintenance and operations was directly affecting the quality and quantity of the product.

Production line operators and maintenance staff were working extra shifts to meet orders, and the costs of overtime and maintenance-related repairs were taking a bite out of profits. For an industry that depends on volume to generate profits, this was bad news. After consultation, senior management decided that a change improvement project would be launched immediately to better the work processes for maintenance and operations.

Learned Experiences

To take advantage of past experience, each employee was asked to complete a questionnaire, and the result was a list of opportunities that could help achieve Tiger Cola's key performance targets. Items were categorized by functional area and given to the change management team to support the change initiative.

Establishment

The Steering Committee

The first step in establishment was to create a project steering committee. It was made up of middle-management representatives from the key stakeholder departments: maintenance, operations and quality control. The steering committee's responsibility was to establish the project goals and objectives, key performance indicators, project budget, and a change management team. Members attended weekly project management meetings to ensure the project stayed on schedule and on budget. The committee was also the decision-making group that dealt with project variance and changes in the scope of the project.

The Change Improvement Project

The steering committee established a change improvement project and named it OPt-IMO (Operating Proactively to Increase Market Opportunities).

Project Responsibilities Matrix

In order to set up the change management team, a project responsibilities matrix was used. With my support, the steering committee established the required tasks and determined who best would be assigned the responsibility. The following is an example of the management matrix and some task responsibility assignments:

OPt-IMO CHANGE IMPROVEMENT PROJECT TASK ASSIGNMENT RESPONSIBILITY MATRIX	Raymond	Smith	Atwater	Jones	Campbell	Archibald
Develop workflow chart		R				
Develop operational guidelines	R					
Develop maintenance guidelines				R		
Establish new equipment strategies				R		
Review equipment replacements			R			
Develop training plan					R	
Develop logistics plan						R
Develop orientation and roll-out plan						R
Establish training facilities					R	

The Role of the Consultant

As the consultant, my role was to support the steering committee and lead the change management team on an as-needed basis for this project.

Project Goals and Objectives

The change management team established the following project goals and objectives with support from upper management and me:

PROJECT GOALS

- Complete the development phase steps by the end of the first quarter 2001

- Complete the implementation phase steps by the end of the second quarter 2001

- Train all production employees in new practices by the end of the second quarter 2001

- Complete the project within the established budget

- Implement a continuous improvement process by the end of the third quarter 2001

PROJECT OBJECTIVES

- Assign the change management team full-time during the development phase

- Assign the change management team part-time during the implementation phase

- Establish an orientation and training program during the first quarter 2001

- Use project management software to manage the project tasks, costs and schedule

- Meet weekly to review project status

- Identify variance in project status and determine solutions if variance is negative (over budget, behind schedule, etc.)

Key Performance Targets

Based on the project goals and the data from the business process assessment survey, key performance targets were established for each of the functional areas:

MAINTENANCE

- An emergency workload representing less than 5% of total workload

- An urgent workload representing less than 10% of total workload

- Measurable preventive maintenance work orders representing more than 65% of total work orders

- 58% of workers' time spent on direct hands-on related duties (indirect duties including training, meetings, breaks, lunch and clean up account for almost 40% of a worker's daily routine)

- An inventory of only critical spare parts

OPERATIONS

- 98% line throughput efficiency

QUALITY CONTROL

- A non-conforming product rate of less than 2%

Budget and Cost Control

A budget was established and approved based on the project timeline, the support resources available and the indirect support requirements. A breakdown of budget areas and calculations to achieve the final project control budget was established as follows:

RESOURCES

- Management salaries attributed to the project commitment
- Employees' hourly rate attributed to training

INDIRECT SUPPORT REQUIREMENTS

- Change management consultant
- Office space, equipment, materials, etc.
- Training facilities, equipment and materials
- A new software package for maintenance

Project Milestone Schedule

The tasks outlined in the responsibilities matrix were entered into the project management software, along with resources, durations and start/finish times.

Vision Statement

Each member of the change management team was involved in the development of the vision statement, which communicated the intent of the project and expected results. It read: *"Our vision*

is to enjoy 80% of market share with earnings per share of $2.50 by successfully changing our production and maintenance practices."

Mission Statement

The change management team developed a mission statement with input from each member of the maintenance department and from a representative from each of the other stakeholder departments. The intention was to provide a simple explanation of the maintenance philosophy:
"The mission of the Maintenance Department is to provide proactive servicing of equipment for their Production customer so as to maximize the quantity and quality of product produced." A similar mission statement was developed for all departments to clearly state their promise to deliver a best-practice level of service to ensure the project vision was achieved.

Communication

Communication meetings were held each Thursday at 10:00 A.M. so that the team could review and update the status of the project. Results of the meeting were posted on the company bulletin boards and distributed as memos to each stakeholder department. A special monthly meeting was held to update senior management on the progress and status of the project.

Change Management Training

Before the OPt-IMO team embarked on the change project, a workshop was held to instruct middle managers and the change management team members in successful change management theories and practices.

Development Phase

Methodology

The change management methodology of key deliverables, objectives and strategies was applied to each process, policy, guideline, procedure and program identified as part of the project. These were developed and designed by the individuals assigned by the project responsibility matrix.

Design

As part of the development phase design step, a maintenance philosophy and strategy were developed:

Maintenance Philosophy

Tiger Cola viewed the maintenance department as being responsible for maintaining equipment and facilities in a manner that assured the required capacity to meet the production goals of the facility and requirements of the operations department. The operations department was considered the owner of the equipment it operated, and as the owner, it was responsible for operating the equipment in a manner that minimized required maintenance. It was also responsible for cooperating with the maintenance department to make the equipment available in accordance with the daily maintenance schedule.

Maintenance Strategy

The organization's focus was on establishing and managing a 52-week business and inspection schedule for all equipment and major components. Major component overhauls were to be performed using Original Equipment Manufacturer shops wherever feasible. Maintenance activities were scheduled so that

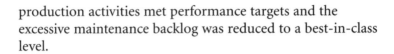

production activities met performance targets and the excessive maintenance backlog was reduced to a best-in-class level.

A maintenance management flowchart reflected the activities and actions to be performed according to a work order process that was managed by priority and status codes. This strategy allowed all work to be identified, planned, scheduled, executed and controlled providing the level of service required by the maintenance department. In turn, this process supported the maintenance mission statement of delivering a service to their customer—the production department—in a timely and effective manner. The key elements of the work order process are briefly explained below.

Work Identification

A process was established to identify the need for equipment and the level of maintenance necessary to achieve the targeted performance requirements.

Work Planning

A process to develop a job plan specified the instructions, materials, personnel, tools, equipment, and procedures for each task to be done.

Work Scheduling

The identified and planned work was laid out in a specific sequence to utilize available resources as productively as possible, while still meeting the expectations of the person requesting the maintenance services.

Work Execution

A means of accomplishing the work included reviewing the scope of the job with all personnel involved; acquiring the necessary tools, materials and parts; confirming equipment availability; and completing the scheduled work activities, including managing any change to the execution schedule.

Work Follow-up

A follow-up process documented the completed work, including comparing the actual execution to the plan, recording repair data in the equipment history file and requesting technical follow-up to improve the maintenance activity.

Performance Analysis

Preventive, predictive and proactive technologies were developed to identify situations that led to equipment failure and control them as much as possible. An ongoing review process was established to optimize the resources applied to maintenance as well as the maintenance strategies associated with equipment upkeep.

Reference Manual

A reference manual was created as part of the overall business process, acting as the "Maintenance Management Bible" for ongoing reference and training.

Implementation Phase

Orientation and Training

Orientation

The business owner scheduled a half-day meeting for everyone directly involved in implementing the change improvement project and a two-hour orientation session for everyone indirectly affected. The orientation objective was to emphasize the goals of the project and to demonstrate the new business process and its supporting guidelines and procedures prior to roll-out.

Training

Employees involved in creating work orders and managing inventory were trained according to the software vendor's specifications. The remaining training was carried out according to the training plan that developed by one of the change management team members during the development phase. The purpose of this was to train the individuals who were not assigned to the change management team but were nevertheless affected by the change project so they become familiar with the new process and its associated guidelines and procedures. Training took two weeks to complete.

Certification Recognition and Qualification

Production and maintenance employees received certification recognition after six weeks of hands-on coaching and qualifying assessment reviews.

Roll-out

Once the project objectives for the development phase had been met and most of the training was complete, it was time to roll out the new process. This involved introducing the new procedures, work order formats, software, equipment, relocations, and advertising programs.

Management Phase

Control and Coaching

Project Status and Updates

To keep the project on track, the project status was evaluated weekly and status updates were produced.

Coaching

Coaching was the job of each change management team member, with occasional help from me. No special routine was established, but each team member was available to assist other employees as requested. Their constant coaching and positive feedback helped to promote the new order of business.

Key Performance Indicators

As the change improvement project began to yield results, progress toward the established key performance targets was monitored. Key performance indicators continued to show positive results of the change opportunity initiative. Line efficiencies increased to over 75%, while the rate of non-conforming product was reduced by 12%. Production operators wrote more work orders as a proactive measure, resulting in more maintenance activities each week.

Managing Changes to the Scope of Project Work

The only change to the scope of project work worth mentioning was the creation of an additional spare parts area, which did not affect the project budget or schedule.

Continuous Improvement

Learned Experiences

Once the roll-out was complete and the new processes were running successfully, the change management team was renamed the continuous improvement team. Its members were given the responsibility of meeting monthly to review the key performance targets and indicators, looking for any opportunities for further improvement based on this learned experience. Each member of the team was enrolled in a continuous improvement seminar presented by Lister Management Inc.

Continuous Improvement Process

A continuous improvement process was integrated into the business and managed by the new continuous improvement team.

Conclusion

One year after launching the OPt-IMO initiative, equipment reliability and worker performance were being measured regularly and continued to show significant improvement. Production was at an all-time high without any extra shifts being scheduled to meet sales demands. At the end of the project Tiger Cola announced at the project achievement banquet that they would be implementing this change improvement project at each of their manufacturing facilities worldwide. Worker morale had improved, and more projects were established to enhance performance in other departments. Simply by following a defined process, they were able to successfully identify, manage and control change to achieve asset and resource performance excellence.

Chapter 13
Service–A Case Study

"Only the wisest and stupidest of men never change."

Confucius

The sales and service industry is a very dynamic and consumer-dependant industry. Companies must be able to establish strategic plans with the capabilities to react to change at a moment's notice. The following case study provides an overview of how one sales and service company was able to move from a reactive problem to a positive opportunity by successfully managing change.

Background

A long-established car dealership with more than a dozen employees provided sales and services to the people of a small town in Western Canada, population 50,000. Competition for vehicle sales was intense here at the best of times, but had worsened by a recent economic downturn. As a result, the dealership was selling fewer new and used cars, and its vehicle maintenance and repair service became the mainstay of the business.

Corporate Strategy (Strategic Planning)

The dealership owner had not considered establishing a strategic plan in the past. He relied strictly on his business instinct and experience to guide his own future and that of his business. However, it was now becoming obvious that he needed a strategy for developing and managing the dealership to make sure it survived.

He turned to a consulting firm that had a long-term alliance with the automobile manufacturer. The firm conducted a study to provide data for a strategic plan and identify opportunities for change improvement. The consultants assessed geographic location, population by age, number of automobiles by age and type, weather patterns, service types, present and forecast economic situation, current and potential provincial government policies and directions, labor agreements and taxes.

Based on the results of the study, a three-year strategic plan was established.

Planning Phase

Identification

The strategic plan study confirmed that while the competition for vehicle sales was stiff, especially because of the prevailing economic conditions, there was sufficient potential for continued and profitable business in servicing vehicles. That business would have to be earned by providing courteous, prompt, high-quality, value-added service. The owner recognized this and began considering change.

His first step was to schedule an assessment of the service department processes. The same consulting firm interviewed employees and studied current practice guidelines and procedures for vehicle service. It assessed the written procedures and how those procedures were put into practice. It also compared current practices to best practices. The results were categorized by functional area: customer service, vehicle service, parts, accounting, sales and management.

Role of the Consultant

I was hired as a change management consultant on a full-time basis for one month to assist with the development phase of the change improvement project, providing guidance and leadership to the change management team. After that, I worked on a part-time basis to provide orientation and training during the roll-out, and project control and coaching during the management phase.

Establishment

The Change Improvement Project

A change improvement project was established and named "Customer Service Change Improvement Project."

Project Responsibilities Matrix

I established a project responsibilities matrix that identified the tasks required to develop, implement and control the change improvement project. These tasks included the review and redesign of each of the following processes and supporting programs: work order process, parts order process, customer service process and work scheduling process. Advertising programs, inventory management and the training plan were included as well.

The Change Management Team

The change management team consisted of three people assigned to the project full time for the one-month duration, representing customer service, vehicle service and parts. Three others, representing accounting, sales and management, were assigned on an as-needed basis, while I was assigned on a full-time/part-time basis to help develop, implement and control the project.

Goals and Objectives

The change management team established project goals and objectives with support from the owner and from me.

Two key goals were identified:

- Establish a service department that supports three full-time mechanics, two full-time apprentice mechanics and one part-time mechanic and that generates revenues in excess of indirect overhead to allow profit share return annually down to the level of shop floor staff.

- Reduce overhead in the service department to 14 percent by the end of the second quarter 2001.

The change management team established the supporting objectives with my help. Some of the objectives included:

- Enroll customer service and sales department employees in customer service training.

- Develop a new advertising strategy.

- Reorganize the parts department, update to the automobile manufacturer's corporate software for generating work orders and procuring parts, and hold monthly customer appreciation days.

- Update the customer service lounge.

- Develop, implement and manage the change improvement project on time and within budget.

- Communicate project success to employees and customers weekly.

- Establish key performance targets for continued success.

Key Performance Targets

The change management team established the key performance targets for the project. Project costs, duration and implementation success were measured weekly to make sure the primary project goals were being met. If the performance did not meet the established targets, the change management team addressed the problem and identified opportunities to get back on track.

In one weekly meeting it became obvious that the fact that one of the service writers was committed to the project full-time was harming day-to-day operations. To rectify this situation, a retired service writer was brought back on a part-time basis to assist with customer service until the project was completed. This solution provides a perfect example of the business owner taking a leadership role to show his managers how important it was to be committed to the project. This leadership decision would prove to be well worth the risk.

Budget and Cost Control

A change improvement project control budget was set at $63,000, based on the number of individuals assigned to the project, the estimated duration of the project and the indirect costs, which were identified as consulting, software, hardware and office supplies. Then a 10% contingency was added, bringing the estimated cost of the change improvement project to $69,300.

A return-on-investment calculation was based on the premise that there would be enough work to keep three full-time mechanics and two apprentice mechanics busy with vehicle repairs for a minimum of seven months. According to this calculation, any sales of new or used cars would be over and above the return on investment.

Ongoing indirect costs—operating overhead, inventory, taxes, clerical and support resources, office supplies, advertising, utilities, benefits, insurance, etc.—were assessed to make sure they contributed to the business, and every opportunity to eliminate wasted effort and resources was taken.

To control the cost of the project, the budget figure of $69,300 was entered into the project management software, where it was updated on a weekly basis. Actual project costs exceeded the estimate on only one occasion, early in the project.

Project Management

I entered the tasks associated with the project responsibilities matrix in the project management software. Start, finish durations and resources were assigned. The project was scheduled, and a baseline snapshot of the schedule was saved to track and control project status and cost/schedule variance.

An updated bar chart of the project schedule was printed and posted on the bulletin boards each week. I used the project management software to monitor the status of each task and issued status reports to each member of the change management team at the weekly project update meeting. Status and progress charts were generated and posted on the bulletin boards and distributed to the owner and managers for review and approval.

Vision Statement

The change management team defined the vision statement for the project with my support and the support of shop floor staff. It read simply, but effectively: *"Establish a defined process within six months to fully support our mission objectives of Quality, Value Added and Courteous Service to ensure customer satisfaction and return business."*

The project vision statement was posted on each bulletin board for the duration of the project.

Another vision statement was created with input from every employee meet the established goals (key performance targets) of the business. It read: *"Our vision is to provide our customers with a level of service excellence that will ensure their continued business, and that of their friends and family."*

This vision statement was proudly displayed in the customer service and sales departments. The ability to measure performance based on the stated mission could be easily accomplished by tracking the number of repeat customers. A customer feedback form was initiated and provided additional supporting information to measure performance.

Mission Statement

Since a mission statement is created to ensure the ongoing performance of a business, it too had to be measurable by customer response. The statement that was developed by the change management team read:

"Our mission is to provide Quality, Value Added and Courteous Service to fully satisfy each and every customer's requirements within the promised cost estimate and timeframe."

It's worth noting here that the vision and mission were not simply motherhood statements. Each was clearly measurable. Customers could challenge both statements if the business failed to live up to the stated promises.

Development Phase

Methodology

Establish Key Deliverables (What)

The change management team representatives assigned the responsibility established key deliverables for all project tasks. For example, the work order system was to be redesigned, since the current practice was cumbersome and time consuming for both the service writer and the customer. The individual assigned the responsibility for improving the work order process was the service writer herself. Her first task was to establish the key deliverables for the new process—what the process must deliver:

- The work order should be computer generated

- It should take no more than 2 minutes to generate a work order

- Historical information must be available for repeat customers to shorten the time required to record their personal information and the information pertaining to their vehicle

- Cost estimates by work type must be predefined; i.e., brake jobs, oil changes, transmission overhauls, etc.

- The system must be able to generate a date-driven preventive maintenance indicator that prompts the service writer to call previous customers, reminding them that it is time to service their vehicle

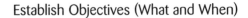

Establish Objectives (What and When)

To achieve the key deliverables for the work order process, and all other processes, it was necessary to establish a number of objectives. For example:

- Purchase a computerized work order management system within the next two months

Determine Strategies (How, Who, Where)

Achieving objectives involved creating strategies that defined how objectives would be achieved, who would accomplish them, and where it would be done. For example:

- The service writer will travel to the corporate offices in Ontario and review their corporate work order software in June

Design

Workflow

A business process workflow for the customer service department was designed by the change management team and displayed on the bulletin boards throughout the dealership. The workflow was kept simple and emphasized the sequence of activities required to efficiently write work orders, procure parts, and provide repair services.

Reference Manual

A reference manual was produced as a reference and training tool. It consisted of a table of contents, control procedures, distribution procedures, workflow illustrations and guidelines and procedures: in essence, it was the *"Customer Service Bible."*

Guidelines and Procedures

Where best-practice procedures where applicable, the guidelines and procedures were re-written to conform. Where benchmark best practices were not available, guidelines and procedures were created to improve current practices. The latter were the most successful because shop floor staff began creating common sense, experience-based procedures.

Implementation Phase

Orientation and Training

Orientation

Once the development and design of the business process and supporting documentation were completed, the business owner scheduled a half-day meeting for everyone affected directly, and a two-hour orientation for those affected indirectly. The orientation objective was to emphasize the goals of the project and demonstrate the new business processes and supporting guidelines and procedures prior to roll-out.

This is the period of change management where the new order of business is accepted or rejected by those directly or indirectly affected. The importance of providing everyone with the details of the project initiative and related materials cannot be emphasized enough. Too many companies have spent hundreds of resource hours and finances on developing new practices but fell short on implementing them due to a lack of buy-in by those affected. Remember, the first step in implementing successful change is to make those affected as comfortable with the new

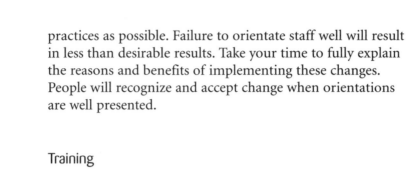

practices as possible. Failure to orientate staff well will result in less than desirable results. Take your time to fully explain the reasons and benefits of implementing these changes. People will recognize and accept change when orientations are well presented.

Training

Training was required for individuals involved in the creation of work orders and inventory management according to the software vendor specifications. The remaining training was carried out according to the training plan established during the development phase by one of the change management team members. The purpose of this was to train everyone affected by the change on the new programs, process and associated guidelines and procedures. Training took two weeks to complete.

Certification Recognition and Qualification

Certification recognition was a direct result of training. Each person who attended training workshops was presented with a certificate of recognition. These certificates were proudly displaced in the services area.

Qualification was a direct result of hands-on coaching, which took place over a period of time following roll-out.

Roll-out

Once the project objectives for the development phase had been met and most of the training completed, it was time to roll out the new processes and supporting guidelines and procedures. This involved introducing new procedures, work order formats, software, equipment, relocations, and advertising programs.

Management Phase

Control and Coaching

Project Status and Updates

During the entire change improvement project, each task was monitored and controlled using project management software and techniques. Each week the results of development and implementation were measured and corrected. Budget and progress were carefully measured to ensure successful change. I assisted with managing the project status and suggested adjustments to any task that was not completed according to the established project plan.

Coaching

Coaching was the job of each change management team member with assistance from me. No special routine was established except that each team member was available to assist other employees as requested. The process of cultivating a new order was assisted through constant coaching and positive feedback.

Key Performance Indicators

As results of the project began to show, the established key performance targets were monitored. Key performance indicators continued to be positive.

Managing Project Scope of Work Changes

Very few changes to the project scope were made during the project cycle. Additional funding was required for training purposes, but this didn't affect the timeline of development and implementation.

Performance

Performance was directly related to the key performance targets and indicators. As the customer service and sales departments began to show an increase in business activity, the performance of each activity remained steady.

Continuous Improvement

Learned Experiences

The change management team was renamed the continuous improvement team and given the responsibility of meeting monthly to review the key performance targets and indicators (mission) and to review any opportunities for further improvement from learned experiences. Each member of the team was enrolled in a continuous improvement seminar established by the corporate automobile manufacturer.

Conclusion

The resulting changes created an opportunity to hire an additional mechanic. As well, it clearly showed that one service writer was enough to fulfil the tasks involved in the new customer service process, so a part-time service writer was relocated to work scheduling and parts preparation.

At the conclusion of the change improvement project, a significant number of changes had been made. The most important achievements were reducing the amount of wasted resources and staff effort and increasing the response time and attention given to each customer. Every member of the organization realized the value in fulfilling the mission and made every effort to continuously improve current business processes and practices.

The resulting change in customer service attracted many new customers as word of service excellence spread. The turnaround time for vehicle maintenance became the mainstay of this company's business. Soon after the implementation of service excellence, the dealership was awarded a special honor by the manufacturer for its achievements.

Chapter 14
Personal Change–A Case Study

"To not seek opportunities is unusual,
to not recognize an opportunity is unfortunate.
To not seize an opportunity is inconceivable."

E. J. Lister

If you're undertaking personal change, it's not necessary to follow every step of the Change Management Process Model.™ A simpler version that includes a personal planning form is adequate, as you'll see in this final case study. For personal change to be successful the essential steps are to identify opportunities for improvement, establish goals and objectives, determine strategies and tasks, and of course monitor performance.

I've included this personal case study to help both employers and employees who want to achieve personal performance excellence. But there are other benefits as well. Companies are only now beginning to recognize that when their employees understand how to manage change in their own life the results are twofold. First, they are more content and productive in conducting the roles and responsibilities of their position, and second, they are better equipped to handle change in the workplace.

Background

Rick (pseudonym) was a 36-year-old production supervisor for a mid-sized manufacturing company at their Western Canadian operation. I first met him at our son's first soccer game in 1994. Rick was a husband, father of two school-aged children, assistant coach of the neighborhood soccer team and a good friend and neighbor.

Rick and his wife had acquired most of the personal assets typical of a young family—suburban home, appliances, furniture and vehicles, as well as a few luxuries such as a camper, boat, and an assortment of sports equipment. Not everything was paid for: each month there were mortgage and car payments to make. Rick and his wife both worked full time. There was enough money coming in to cover expenses, but they weren't able to establish a healthy savings account. However, they were happy, healthy and financially comfortable, and each assumed life would continue on that way.

Planning Phase

Identification

Rick had no long-range plan for his personal life. He had some money put away in a retirement fund, but for the most part the family was living day to day. Like most people without a plan, Rick found himself reacting to change instead of proactively preparing for it.

Caught up in his daily routine, Rick didn't know about his employer's problem holding market share. To maintain acceptable profit and earning ratios, the company decided to reduce the number of front-line supervisors. Rick didn't have a lot of seniority, so he was given a small compensation package and let go.

Thanks to external change he hadn't foreseen, his comfortable lifestyle was at risk. This was a serious problem, but Rick understood it could also be an opportunity if he approached it the right way.

Establishment

The Change Improvement Project

Rick launched his personal change opportunity initiative by completing a personal planning form that I'd developed which allowed him to create a plan—including establishing his goals, defining his objectives, and determining his strategies—and then record and update his progress on a regular basis. Also, it allowed him to measure his performance accurately using a checklist to monitor his completed tasks.

As we've discussed, the change improvement project is a roadmap, showing where you are, where you want to go, and where you should be at any given time. Rick identified his goals and assigned each objective a start-time, duration period and finish-time. He understood that overachieving on his objectives was fine, so long as it didn't shortchange other aspects of the project. Underachieving was an opportunity to get back on course.

The Personal Planning Form

On the following page is an example of the personal planning form Rick used to establish his plan.

DIAGRAM: Personal Planning Form

Name: Rick Pseudonym	Date: April 12, 2000
Goal: When? (Must be realistic and measurable)	
Establish a career in Computer Aided Design	
Establish a savings account and maintain a minimum of $3,500.00	
Objectives: What? – (Steps I will take to achieve my goals) and When?	
Objective 1: Create a new resumé before May 6, 2000.	
Objective 2: Find interim employment as soon as possible, (preferably in Computer Aided Design, but not essential).	
Objective 3: Enroll in part-time evening class training in Computer Aided Design this summer.	
Objective 4: Establish a budget and savings plan today.	
Strategies to achieve my objectives: Who? How? Where?	
Strategy 1: Create a new resumé by using the online resumé builder on my computer at home.	
Strategy 2: Post my resumé on internet employment websites and mail out to potential employers. Search the newspaper and employment agencies for work.	
Strategy 3: Go to the local college and apply for part-time evening class training.	
Strategy 4: Go to our bank and ask for assistance and information on establishing a budget and saving plan.	

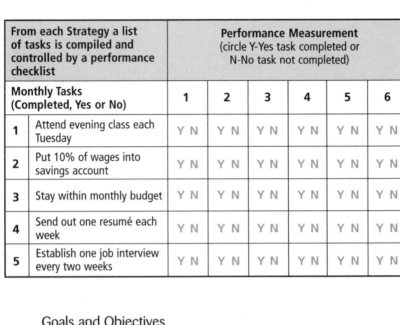

From each Strategy a list of tasks is compiled and controlled by a performance checklist	Performance Measurement (circle Y-Yes task completed or N-No task not completed)					
Monthly Tasks (Completed, Yes or No)	**1**	**2**	**3**	**4**	**5**	**6**
1 Attend evening class each Tuesday	Y N	Y N	Y N	Y N	Y N	Y N
2 Put 10% of wages into savings account	Y N	Y N	Y N	Y N	Y N	Y N
3 Stay within monthly budget	Y N	Y N	Y N	Y N	Y N	Y N
4 Send out one resumé each week	Y N	Y N	Y N	Y N	Y N	Y N
5 Establish one job interview every two weeks	Y N	Y N	Y N	Y N	Y N	Y N

Goals and Objectives

Rick's main goal was to establish a true career. Although his previous position was rewarding in some ways, he'd never considered it a life-long vocation. His real passion was technical design, so he decided this was his opportunity to make a career out of it. He felt working as a technical designer could make him and his family comfortable in the three important areas of his life: health, relationships and finances.

To achieve this goal Rick established only a few key objectives:

- Find interim employment (preferably in Computer Aided Design, but this wasn't essential)
- Enroll in part-time training for Computer Aided Design
- Create a new resumé
- Approach potential employers for jobs related to Computer Aided Design
- Establish a savings plan

Key Performance Targets

Rick knew that once he achieved his goals, he would need a method of maintaining the results: keeping the new job and earning enough money to give his family a comfortable lifestyle. This meant maintaining his key performance targets related to financial savings, budgeting and upgrading his skills through part-time education. The most important goal was adding money regularly to the family savings account. Any failure to make a contribution had to be justified and managed.

Budget and Cost Control

Rick used a budget and cost control process to support his objectives and keep him financially stable throughout the course of the project. This meant limiting family spending on groceries, entertainment and clothing.

The Vision Statement

Rick did not consider establishing a vision statement. He acknowledged later, however, that having a vision statement to support his goals and objectives would have helped him throughout the Change Management Process. If he had established one, it would most likely have been something like: *"I will achieve a comfortable lifestyle for me and the people around me through personal change management."*

The Mission Statement

The personal mission statement that Rick established to support his goals and objectives also provided ongoing guidance. It simply stated: *"My mission is to maintain an established lifestyle that contributes to the physical, emotional and financial heath and wellness of my family, and contributes wherever possible to benefit others ... every day."*

Continuous Improvement

Once Rick recognized the rewards of achieving his stated mission, he began to improve on it by continuing to upgrade his skills through evening courses and increasing his monthly contribution to his savings plan. As an added bonus, he was able to pass on this method of managing change to his fellow employees as well as his employer. He created several change improvement initiatives within his workplace and gradually established himself as an important asset to the company.

Conclusion

Rick was successful in managing change for two reasons: he understood the process of change, and he recognized a problem as a potential opportunity. Through his use of successful change management tools and information, he not only survived and adapted to change, but also improved the quality of his own life environment and the life environment of his entire family.

One year after receiving the news of his termination, Rick was not only back on his feet, he was far ahead of where he would have been had he remained employed as a front-line supervisor. Today Rick is employed as a Computer Aided Design Technician for a major manufacturer that produces automobiles in Southern Ontario. He is able to establish his own opportunities and life strategies to avoid sudden reactive change, and he's prepared to manage any reactive change that might once again sneak up on him. In essence, he has found a way to manage and control his life while continuing to improve his own performance as well as the performance of his finances and family relationships.

PART V   APPENDIX

Dealing with Sudden Change

You can only plan and anticipate so much—unexpected, sudden change can still occur. When it does happen, it's often difficult to recognize it as an opportunity at first. The event or situation could be an immediate problem with no resolution in sight, or it could be a loss of someone or something that can never be replaced. In these situations, you'll go through a period of time when coping with this change requires more than just the written word of an enthusiastic author. Therefore, I encourage you to read the following section—for what it's worth—but also to seek professional counseling if need be.

I have found myself dealing with unexpected, sudden changes on several occasions in my life. There were times when I was laid-off and couldn't find employment in a volunteer soup kitchen. Times when my bank account was so low the bank wanted to charge me for not having any money in it. Then there was the tragedy of losing my father to cancer at the same time that my children were wondering why I didn't live with them anymore. Although some of these sudden changes could have been prevented had I established a personal long-range plan, some events and situations simply blind-sided me. But I survived, and in most cases I became stronger as a result of it.

> Every adversity, every failure and every threat
> carries with it the seed of an equivalent or
> greater benefit.

A promotion, demotion or change in job assignments, an illness, disability or death in the family, divorce or relationship problems are some of life's real events that fall into the category of "unexpected, sudden change."

Professionals say we cope with this kind of change in much the same way we cope with grief. When it is first identified, we generally experience some level of emotional trauma. The change appears to threaten our sense of security, and we feel a loss of control.

In an attempt to gain back control and feel secure again, we enter a state of denial. We say things like "I can't believe that this is happening to me." But because it is happening and because we're powerless to reverse it, disbelief turns to anger. Eventually sadness and depression replaces anger as we recognize that our anger won't give us back the control we've lost. The grieving process ends when we finally accept the event or situation.

While it may not be possible to reverse the events that caused this uncomfortable, often painful, process, it is possible to manage how the change ultimately affects us. To help recover from unexpected, sudden change and strengthen your character, professionals recommend trying the following ways of coping.

Ways of Coping

Strengthen Your Self-Confidence

Research shows that the more confidence people have in themselves and their abilities, the better they manage life's changes. What are you doing to build your confidence? Are you establishing a plan? Are you silencing your pathological, critical inner-voice and replacing it with a little voice trained to say positive things? Find a confidence-builder and develop it. I've found that I can increase my self-confidence by simply talking positively to my inner self and remembering times that I did something well and received recognition for doing so. More often than not I've been able to build my confidence by trying a new recipe. Other times I walk tall and pretend I'm famous.

Perhaps you could challenge yourself to perform something simple that you've never attempted before. Group activities are helpful as well. Toastmasters International is an organization for people who wish to learn public speaking. Attending their sessions gave me more confidence than Hercules. Their positive reinforcement and proven techniques can make you a new and improved person. It worked for me.

If You Know Change is Coming, Do Something

Slow, eventual changes are the easiest to manage. If debts are beginning to pile up, take charge of the situation before it worsens. If your company is making several changes—realigning departments, closing down offices, switching computer systems—assess what you need to do to stay on top of the situation and take steps to make it happen. For example, you may decide to prepare by continuing your education or learning a new skill.

Look for Something Positive in the Change

While it's impossible to ignore the downside of some changes, being negative for an extended length of time is not productive. Find something about the change that's positive, focus on it, and put the negative aspects of the situation into perspective. I read somewhere that opportunity come one step past the point where most people accept failure. The reason for this is we pay so much attention to the problem that we're not keeping our eyes open for the opportunity.

Build on Your Support System

A close network of friends and family members can help you weather life's toughest storms. Gather about you people who are nurturing, who share your life's beliefs and with whom you enjoy spending time. Remember, too, to be there for them when they are struggling with change.

Visualize Your Full Recovery from the Change

Having a mental image of how you'd like things to be can help you feel better more quickly. Picture yourself fully recovered from the change, without any stress or anxiety. How will your life be different? What will you be doing?

Stay in Good Health

Next to support from those you love, good health is your greatest asset. If you smoke, consider quitting. If you don't get enough exercise, start looking for ways to increase your level of physical activity. Assess your diet and look for ways to make it better. Your body has built-in, natural stress fighters that can help you respond positively to change. The time you spend nurturing these stress fighters will improve your situation overall.

Don't Rely on Alcohol or Other Drugs

Drinking or drugging is no way to cope with upsetting events in life. In fact, turning to alcohol or other drugs will only worsen the situation by weakening your ability to respond to change.

Evaluate Your Reaction to Change

Ask yourself what you would do differently next time. Did your reaction to the change surprise you? What did you do that worked well—or didn't work? How would you better prepare yourself next time? Experience is the best teacher.

Handling the Stress of Change

All change is stressful to some degree. But some changes to our personal, work or business environments are more stressful than others, even positive changes like becoming a new mom or dad, or accepting a job promotion.

Because the effects of change can last for several months, it's important to know the signs of excessive stress:

- Difficulty concentrating

- Sleeping less or always feeling tired

- Crying for no apparent reason

- Taking longer than average to recover from common illnesses

- Feeling depressed

- Thinking or talking about suicide

If stress appears to be getting the better of you, try these tips:

Practice Relaxation Exercises

Try taking a deep breath and holding it for five seconds. Then, let it out slowly as you picture all the stress leaving your body. Do this three or four times. Another technique is muscle relaxation. Begin at your toes and slowly work up and down your body, tensing a few muscles at a time and then completely relaxing them.

Exercise, Exercise and Exercise

Your body has natural stress fighters that actually become more effective with exercise. Walking, taking up a sport, swimming, horseback riding—find an exercise routine that you enjoy and begin to feel the benefits.

I can vouch for this as my time spent with horses—both riding and caring for them—does wonders for my stress management, not to mention providing the weight control benefits of hauling manure across six acres of pasture.

Note: If you've had persistent thoughts of suicide, it's time to consult a professional: a doctor, psychiatrist, psychologist, counselor, or social worker.

Summary—Best Practices

This summary is meant to provide you with a quick reference guide to best practices to successfully manage change. If you're not clear on any point, just go back to the appropriate chapter to refresh your memory.

Chapter 1: Understanding Change

Understand change and establish a positive attitude towards it. Learn to see problems as opportunities to maximize your emotional, physical, financial, and/or business well-being.

Chapter 2: Model Overview

Understand the Change Management Process and learn to follow it step-by-step using project management and performance management techniques. This process is the key to successful change.

Chapter 3: Identification

Evaluate and assess current practices in your personal, work or business environments and benchmark them against best practices to identify opportunities for change.

Chapter 4: Establishment

- Establish a change improvement project based on the opportunity you've identified.

- Establish project goals and objectives.

- Establish key performance targets.

- Establish a change management plan.

Chapter 5: Methodology

- Use the methodology described to manage your change project.

- Establish key deliverables.

- Establish strategies for executing and managing each objective.

Chapter 6: Design

Design workflows, guidelines, procedures and programs to support your change improvement project.

Chapter 7: Orientation and Training

Provide orientation and training for everyone who will potentially be affected by the change project to make them familiar with the new guidelines, procedures and programs.

Chapter 8: Roll-out

Roll out the change using a roll-out plan that emphasizes a new and exciting idea, service or product.

Chapter 9: Control and Coaching

Control the status of your change improvement project using project management techniques, and coach employees so that they can perform as well as possible.

Chapter 10: Continuous Improvement

Continually assess the success of your project and look for opportunities to improve.

Chapter 11: The Organizational Impact of Performance Change

Make sure you have the right personnel in the right positions to support the change.

On a Personal Note

The future of every individual or business organization is forever uncertain, except for the fact that death, taxes and constant change will inevitably feature in there somewhere. Most people accept that death and even taxes are certain. However, they often resist change. The irony is that embracing change can help enhance or prolong your life and reduce your taxes. Thinking positively and changing unhealthy habits will produce results that have been proven to add years to your life, or at least make it more pleasurable while you're alive. Reducing taxes may be as easy as starting a business or contributing to tax-deductible retirement savings plans offered by the government.

To ensure successful change is to accept change and feel comfortable with it. By creating a change environment that is acceptable and enjoyable, both individuals and businesses can develop and grow.

This book provides numerous ideas and management tools to assist you in successfully making the change from one practice to another. The intent is to help you change proactively, so that you shift from current practices to best practices. Hopefully some of these changes will not simply equal best practices, but rather, establish the new benchmarks that every other individual or business organization will be measured by.

There are many experts on the subject of change management—and many more change management ideas and tools on the market today. I have tried, however, to focus on the personal aspect of change management and provide a simple process that anyone can use to successfully identify and manage any change opportunity initiative. I sincerely hope you find the content of this book useful in creating an enjoyable change environment that will ultimately provide you with a greater sense of achievement in your personal, work or business environment.

Regards

E.J. (Ted) Lister

About the Author

EDMUND (TED) J. LISTER

With more field experience from the school of hard knocks than formal education, author E.J. (Ted) Lister has successfully managed change in personal, work and business environments, both for himself and his clients. He has spent more than 15 years developing, reengineering and implementing change improvements, establishing himself as someone who can create and control change to establish best-practice performance excellence.

Mr. Lister is the author of several training manuals for industry-related management systems using change management concepts. He has led numerous workshops and seminars at an international level and consults regularly to a wide range of clients, including companies in the petro-chemical, gas processing, bottling, mining and refining industries, with a special interest in their employees' personal and work environments. He has particular expertise in the area of Human Resource Performance and Production Asset Performance.

Mr. Lister lives in the mural town of Chemainus, British Columbia, Canada. He divides his time between writing, consulting, and horseback riding with his partner in life, Patricia (Toonie).

Additional copies of *Successful Change Management* are available on line, or at your local bookstore. For bulk orders, or to arrange author interviews, special events, lectures or in-house instructional workshops, please contact:

> Lister Management Inc.
> 3115 River Road
> Chemainus, British Columbia
> Canada V0R 1K3
> Ph: 250-246-3470 Fax: 250-246-3475
> tlister@listermanagement.com
> order@listermanagement.com *(for book orders)*
> www.listermanagement.com

The following Change Management training, information and tools are available by contacting Lister Management Inc.:

- Change Management Workshop Seminars

- Performance Management Workshop Seminars

- Change Management Facilitator Training *(train the trainer)*

- Project Management for Change Workshop

- Microsoft® Project Workshop Seminars

- Microsoft® Outlook® Workshop Seminars

The following Change Management tools will soon be available on the Lister Management Inc. web portal: **www.listermanagement.com**

- Change Management Discussion Forum

- Change Decision Calculator™

- Receptive-to-Change Questionnaire©

To be notified by email of future Change Management Training Workshops and Seminars, please send your email address to <tlister@listermanagement.com> with *Mailing List* in the subject field. Be assured we will respect your privacy; your email address and contact information will never be provided to any other organizations or individuals.